ON THE

Wings

OF THE

Dawn

Also by Max Meyers

Riding the Heavens

ON THE Wings OF THE Dawn

MORE STORIES OF ADVENTURE TO ENCOURAGE YOUR FAITH

MAX MEYERS

ZONDERVAN

GRAND RAPIDS, MICHIGAN 49530

ZONDERVAN

On the Wings of the Dawn
Copyright © 2001 by Max Meyers

Requests for information should be addressed to:

Zondervan, *Grand Rapids, Michigan 49530*

Library of Congress Cataloging-in-Publication Data

Meyers, Max, 1935-
    On the wings of dawn : more stories of adventure to encourage your faith /
Max Meyers.
       p. cm.
    Includes bibliographical references.
    ISBN 0-310-23334-8 (hardcover : alk. paper)
    1. Meyers, Max, 1935-   2. Mission Aviation Fellowship—Biography.
3. Aviation in missionary work.   I. Title.
BV2082.A9 M485 2001
266'.0092—dc21
   [B]   2001017679

This edition printed on acid-free paper.

Published in association with the literary agency of Alive Communications, Inc., 7680 Goddard Street, Suite 200, Colorado Springs, CO 80920.

Interior design by Beth Shagene
Printed in the United States of America

01 02 03 04 05 06 07 08 /❖ DC/ 10 9 8 7 6 5 4 3 2 1

If I rise on the wings of the dawn,
  If I settle on the far sides of the sea,
Even there your hand will guide me,
  Your right hand will hold me fast.

Psalm 139:9–10

CONTENTS

*To Jo, my life partner
and traveling companion for forty-two years.*

*To Michael, Timothy, Jonathan, Robin, and Christopher,
sons who make me feel so proud.*

*To the special friends and colleagues of Development
Associates International, committed to the strategic role of
developing integrity and effectiveness among leaders.*

*To the people of Mission Aviation Fellowship,
with whom I have been privileged to work over
the greater part of my life.*

*To the countless thousands whom I have met along the way
all over this amazing world, particularly those from
other cultures who in many ways have blessed my life
and broadened my understanding of God.*

I am grateful to you all.

ACKNOWLEDGMENTS

I have simply written stories! Experiences gathered over the years. In doing so I have received an incredible amount of help, for which I am deeply grateful. There is Jo, of course, and our son Tim, who have both spent countless hours at polishing and refining the manuscript. There is Rosalie and our son Jon, whose input was very valuable. Then there are my editor friends John Sloan and Bob Hudson and, among my many encouragers, Joyce and Ghislaine. I couldn't have done this without them.

But if these are nothing but stories, I have failed. I've tried to present them as parables, stories with a deeper meaning, following the theme of making choices. I hope you see this. I hope that you read these stories and find God. May he be central in your decision-making, at your crossroads.

Teaching with parables was the masterstroke of genius that Jesus used so effectively. My ultimate goal will be achieved if in these stories you find him.

Chapter

1

WOOLFIE, CAESAR, AND ME

Airplanes fascinate little boys.

Ask a little boy to draw something for you, and he'll probably draw an airplane. It may not be a startling breakthrough in aviation design, but he'll tell you what it is. He'll draw the pilot, and most likely it'll be him. Or his dad.

I could draw wonderful pictures of airplanes.

All the kids on my street, like most little boys, at some time or other, dreamed of being pilots. For them, the dream didn't last. But among those for whom the dream to fly does become real, there is a unique bond.

Growing up, I was captivated by the words of John Gillespie Magee Jr., a "missionary kid" born in China, who at the tender age of nineteen, was flying Spitfires during the Battle of Britain in 1941. Just a short time before he was killed in a tragic midair collision, he wrote this classic poem, "High Flight."

Oh! I have slipped the surly bonds of earth
And danced the skies on laughter-silvered wings;
Sunward I've climbed, and joined the tumbling mirth
Of sun-split clouds ... and done a hundred things
You have not dreamed of ... wheeled and soared and swung
High in the sunlit silence. Hov'ring there,
I've chased the shouting wind along, and flung
My eager craft through footless halls of air.

Up, up the long, delirious burning blue
I've topped the wind-swept heights with easy grace
Where never lark, or even eagle flew.
And, while with silent, lifting mind I've trod
The high untrespassed sanctity of space
*Put out my hand, and touched the face of God.**

To fly, I believed, must be the greatest thrill available to man! And that passion for flying crossed the most unlikely boundaries.

Mr. Woolfe, my high school Latin teacher, had been a pilot. He displayed all the symptoms. The faintest hum of a faraway airplane engine would find "Old Woolfie" dashing to the nearest window, gazing skyward, straining to see. It was a habit I well understood and a weakness I learned to exploit. I could usually devise a question about Woolfie's previous career in the air that would lure him away from the task at hand. The whole class could then lean back to enjoy a few minutes respite as we listened to another story from this old air warrior. Mr. Woolfe found teaching very second-rate. In his heart, he was still up in the air.

"Old Woolfie" was Woolfe by name and wolf by nature! He was tough. In the immaturity of youth I almost hated him,

*"High Flight" by John Gillespie Magee Jr. is used here by permission of IHT corporation.

though I know it must have been difficult teaching a herd of lively, recalcitrant boys a language that we thought belonged only to antiquity.

Old Woolfie demanded absolute attention. While he would go to the window to identify an airplane, he would not brook the slightest distraction by a class member. Latin was *never* fun. There was no carrot to entice us. But there certainly was a stick.

Caesar's Gaelic Wars, a bloodthirsty tale of the exploits of Julius Caesar, was Old Woolfie's stick. For a boy of thirteen, to be forced to translate this tome into English was tantamount to child abuse.

"You're talking again, Meyers," he would shout as he caught me whispering to my neighbor. "The next chapter of Caesar by tomorrow morning!"

"Hang it!" I'd mutter to myself. "There goes cricket in the street! There goes all my free time until tomorrow." I'm convinced I did more translation of that wretched book than any other kid in the entire school. I think I knew more about Caesar's military strategy than did Caesar himself! Perhaps for some boys on the brink of manhood, interminable processions of impedimenta and catapults, Romans in white togas, chariots, slaves, and vassals might be of compelling interest, but to me, cricket with my mates had more to offer.

Old Woolfie was also a trusting soul. And methodical. He would begin every class by dealing with unfinished business from the previous day. On any given morning, following the imposing of extra homework as a punishment, he would say, "All the boys with impositions from yesterday, stand up. Show me your translation of Caesar, Meyers." It became such a regular occurrence that he didn't even bother to collect my work. I guess his desk drawer was full of chapters I had already translated. He would just ask me to show it to him—hold it up from where I stood at my desk, as near to the back of the class as I could possibly get. Strangely, while I was sure he disliked me, he trusted me.

"Why do all this work?" I would think to myself as the impositions were coming thick and fast. I was translating a couple of chapters of Caesar every week. Woolfie and I had a genuine old-time feud going on. A battle of wills. So one day I took advantage of his trust, and when I had to show my chapter of the *Gaelic Wars*, I confidently held up three or four pages I had carefully torn out of my previous year's history notebook.

And I got away with it. He didn't ask to see my work. And he failed to notice I hadn't torn it up as requested. After all, why destroy it? I could use it again. And again. And again. I could never have imagined that last year's history notes were of such inestimable value.

It was a great plan. It went on for weeks. Cricket after school. Evenings of freedom. Mine again to enjoy!

Unfortunately, my pride was my undoing. Had I kept my artful dodging to myself, it might have remained undetected. But it's not the way of boys to keep such things to themselves. I made the big mistake of telling a couple of mates how clever I was. They were impressed. It all caught up with me one day. Seeing smirks on the faces of some of the class when he requested my latest "translation," Old Woolfie became suspicious. "Bring it out here, Meyers, I want to see your work." There were audible gasps. I tried to convince him from my position of refuge at the back of the room that he really didn't need to see it as, by this time, I was becoming quite the *Gaelic War* scholar. He was unconvinced.

Reluctantly I forfeited my prized, well-worn history notes.

He stood there quietly for a moment or two, reading. His face reddened. His eyes bulged. My brief life was over. I knew it! Then, while the entire class listened in awed silence, he delivered his address. It was a verbal thrashing—about deception, betrayal of trust, about downright dishonesty and cowardice. Then came his final verdict.

"Meyers," he scowled, "after all these years teaching young boys like you, I have become an excellent judge of character. I have seen many of my boys through to adulthood. I've always been right, Meyers. I've known where they'll end up. And I have seen you every day, Meyers, as I have taught you now for two years. You refuse to treat this subject seriously. And this is an unconscionable betrayal of my trust. You influence other boys in your downward spiral of behavior and attitude. And I know, Meyers, I know where you're headed. Prison! Prison is the ultimate place for delinquents like you. You'll be in jail one day, Meyers. Jail!

I was ridden with guilt. Ashamed and embarrassed, I had deeply hurt the old bloke.

Mr. Woolfe and I never spoke again at school. Not surprisingly, I found myself in another Latin class! Upon reflection, I doubt whether either of us regretted that. He wasn't a bad teacher. He just had a terrible subject to teach.

It was ten years later when I next saw Mr. Woolfe. I was standing in uniform at Sydney's Central Station, waiting for a train. By then, I was an Air Force fighter pilot. And there he was. I could hardly believe it was him. He looked older, but it was Old Woolfie in person. Should I speak to him? I wasn't sure.

"Prison, Meyers. That's where you'll end up. . . ."

Hmmm.

I braced myself and walked up to him. "Hello, Mr. Woolfe. It's really nice to see you."

Immediately his face lit up. He looked at my uniform and the pilot's wings on my chest. He stared at my face, quizzically. "I don't remember your name. Your face is familiar, though. Did I teach you at school? An Air Force pilot! That's wonderful! Who are you, Son?" he said, as he pumped my hand enthusiastically.

I gulped!

"I'm Max Meyers, sir," I said. "Canterbury High School. '49."

"Oh, yes, Meyers," he said. He continued to shake my hand vigorously. "I remember you now! Clearly! And you've become an Air Force pilot, huh? So, tell me all about it. What sort of airplanes do you fly?

"I'm with 75 Squadron, sir, flying Meteors."

"Meteors! Oh, how I envy you." He was genuinely pleased, overjoyed to speak with me.

"How does it feel to fly a jet fighter? You must have worked hard to get where you are, son."

He said numerous times that he felt so proud to have been a part of my education!

We talked on together—not about Latin, just about airplanes! It was great to chat with him.

His final comment said it all:

"You know, Meyers, even all those years ago, I knew you had what it took! I knew you would end up doing something great! I could see it in you, Meyers. You had it in you, Son—right from the start! I knew my boys!"

I was pretty pleased with myself as I spoke with him. Yes, my dreams had been fulfilled. But I had been such a fool during those crucial high school years. Wasted opportunities have their peculiar cost. Learning Latin was, of course, a relatively small thing. But in trying to be smart and enjoying my rebellion, I had denied myself at least the beginnings of a more classical education. And I've always regretted that.

———

Perhaps my life—and yours—could have taken an entirely different direction at some point or another if such opportunities had not been wasted. So many of our roadblocks are self-created. But I stand in awe, and I hope you do too, of God's grace in steering and guiding lives into effectiveness and useful service for him.

He takes the crayon sketches of a little kid—and makes them brushstrokes on the perfect canvas of his eternal purpose. He takes childhood fascinations and dreams, youthful ambitions—and makes them fly.

From time to time I think of Old Woolfie, and especially of that last meeting. I recall how warmly he shook my hand and how genuinely glad he was to see me.

But I'd love to think that he really did remember me!

Whoever loves discipline loves knowledge, but he who hates correction is stupid.

PROVERBS 12:1

THE STUFF OF DREAMS

Life can be pretty boring for a kid.

But sometimes, gloriously unexpected things happen.

Such was the day for me when I took my first ride in an airplane.

From earliest childhood I had turned my eyes to the sky at the sound of every plane. In the forties our family lived in "safe" Sydney. The most we saw of World War II were the aircraft that flew overhead. I loved to hear the screaming howls of their engines. I loved to watch as they practiced their incredible dog-fight maneuvers high above. From the ground they were black specks against the blue. But there were men up there. And I was a boy. And it all seemed great adventure to me.

I clearly recall one particular day when my brothers and I sat under the wing of a gray-green Dakota at Sydney's Mascot Airport. It was parked with two others, right by the fence on the far boundary. Each of them bore the insignia of the Royal Dutch Air Force. The crew members appeared to have little to do but lounge around by their aircraft. Only young men, their stories amazed us. Evading the Japanese army as it stormed its way through Java, down toward Australia, they had flown from the Dutch East Indies and were simply hanging out, far from home, awaiting reassignment. We sat open-mouthed, listening to their tales.

In the evenings, with our parents, we crowded around the radio as Dad twiddled the dial to catch, through the crackle and static, the news of the war. We heard of the exploits of men like these—in New Guinea and other war zones in the Pacific region.

Airplanes—flying! Unbelievable adventure. Uniformed men with wings on their chests. The heroes of the day.

To fly! This was the stuff of dreams.

And then the war was over and life slowly returned to normal. On my street, dads and elder brothers returned. Most of them.

The decade drew to a close. There were very few military planes to watch anymore. The gray-green Dakotas of wartime had become the shiny silver airliners that now flew overhead. But dreams never die.

I thought my dad was the best dad on the street. But he was always busy. He worked long hours, and it seemed that there were so many things that needed his attention, especially on weekends. There were few family outings. And family vacations were rare. There was no time, and no extra money. On a Saturday, he could be something of a slave driver, demanding our help to get those jobs done. We, of course, would rather have been skinny-dipping in the forbidden quarry or smoking home-rolled newspaper cigarettes in our secret hiding place underneath the wooden floor of the local church.

Sundays were "church days." Church in the morning. Church in the afternoon. Church at supper time. It seemed to me that we were a "churched-out" family!

Then one day, late in 1949, Dad announced that he had been able to get some time off from work and was planning to take the family away on holiday. It was to be at a place he had often talked about, by the beach. There would be sand hills to climb, bush to explore! We could swim at either the surf beach or in a still-water lake behind the sand hills. It sounded absolutely fantastic.

But after supper, my parents said to me, "Hey, Max, don't leave the table yet. We need to talk with you about this holiday." I was a little apprehensive. Special talks usually involved reprimand or punishment. But this time there was no hint of impending trouble for me in their voices, rather, a sympathetic tone.

"This is going to be really tough on you, Son" my dad said, "You'll have to stay at home while we take the other kids on this holiday. The only vacation time I can get is right when you'll be doing the Intermediate Exam. Any other year it wouldn't matter quite as much, but this year it's different. You just can't be away. I've tried hard to change the dates, but it simply isn't possible. You'll have to stay here with Grandma while we're gone."

There was genuine sadness in their eyes as they told me how much they had tried to make it work for us all to be together.

Stay at home? Miss such an exciting place? When everyone else was going? The only one of all five kids not to go? I argued with them that the Intermediate Exam wasn't really important. But to no avail. There would be no vacation at all for anyone that year if, because of me, the holiday was cancelled.

I really did understand, and I knew it had to be. But there was mileage to be made out of the situation, so I didn't try to hide my disappointment.

"I promise you, Son, that we'll do something special just for you. Something that will help make up for this. I don't know what it'll be yet, but I promise you it'll be really good." But how could anything make up for missing two weeks at the beach? I couldn't think of anything that could be that special!

I waved them goodbye. That was easy. And Grandma really spoiled me while they were away. She felt bad for me too. It was their coming home that hurt. Their sunburned faces, the stories they recounted, tales of fishing, swimming, exploring—they had had a wonderful time. I sat, feeling excluded, listening enviously. What "special thing" could ever possibly make up for such a loss?

A few weeks passed. The exams were over. Conversation about the marvelous vacation had become sporadic.

Then, one evening, Dad spoke to me. "Max, I've worked out what you and I are going to do. I'm going to take you, in an airplane, to Canberra."

"What?"

I stared at him. Had I heard him correctly? Did he say . . . ? I couldn't believe it! An airplane!

Absolutely nothing could have generated such joy for me. How could they possibly have conceived of an idea so utterly fantastic? My wildest dreams. How could they afford it?

Dad continued. He spoke about Canberra, as if that might be the highlight of this wonderful proposal. "It's the national capital. A city built and designed specifically for that reason. We'll go to Parliament House, to the National War Museum, to the Institute of Anatomy. I've booked the first flight in the day for us and the last flight home. It should be a great time."

Frankly, I didn't care much for parliament houses or war museums. Certainly not for institutes of anatomy. But—to go in an airplane? Wow! Who wouldn't give up two weeks of family vacation for that?

The great day came. Dad had the airline tickets safely in his inside pocket. It was dark when we left home to walk to the bus stop and still dark when we reached the station and caught the train into Sydney. Even now, I can remember my pride as I strutted with my father into the city terminal of Australian National Airways.

"Man!" I thought to myself, "I've got a great dad!"

"The bus in the first bay is for passengers to Canberra," announced the voice on the public address system. I walked out and boarded, the only kid among a group of businessmen. I felt ten feet tall. Even the ride to the airport was exciting. I wanted everyone who saw that airline bus go by to notice me. I was going flying!

And there it stood. That shiny, beautiful Douglas DC3, glistening in the early morning sunlight. A company flag flew from a small mast near the captain's window. "Australian National Airlines" was written in red along the fuselage. Men were loading luggage into its freight bay behind the passenger door. Others fuelled it from a large tanker truck. A uniformed stewardess then walked across the tarmac and stood by the stairway.

What an airplane! It was identical in shape to the old khaki-green Dutch Dakotas that had fascinated us as small boys all those years ago. Only this one was different. This was a flagship. This was unique. This one was mine.

Carpet on the floor. Luxurious leather seats.

The aisle seemed very steep. There were rows of two seats on one side, one on the other. We were shown to our assigned places a little way up the aircraft, just behind the wing. My dad sat by the aisle. The window seat was mine.

I could see such pleasure in Dad's eyes as I poured my excitement over him and thanked him for bringing me on this incredible adventure. How could he have known? Had he and my mum been able to see inside my heart, they could not have found an experience to match this one. What a prize—just for staying home from a family vacation!

The door was closed and all was ready. With a peculiar whine, the right hand propeller began to turn, then there was a loud noise as the engine started. The white smoke that poured out of the cowls was whisked away by the slipstream. Then the other engine started. The plane vibrated, jerked a little, and moved forward. The pilot turned it sharply and began to taxi toward the take-off point.

The stewardess walked up and down the aisle, offering candy to each of the passengers and checking that all seatbelts were securely fastened. We were on our way!

The engines roared. The vibration increased. And with a jerk the take-off roll began. Faster and faster. The steep aisle became level as the tail came up. The grass at the side of the airstrip flashed by, faster and faster, and then—it just dropped away, downward and backward! We were flying!

I'm sure I never even noticed the cold glass as I pressed my face against the window. Soon the horizon on my side of the airplane rose ever higher as the wing came down, and we circled the airport. I could see the outline of Sydney, with its tall buildings, beautiful glistening harbor, the famous Sydney Harbor bridge, and, far away, the ocean.

Flying!

My dad's face was close to mine as we peered out that square window. He had only flown once before, back in the early thirties. It had been from that same airport. He had saved up his pocket money and taken a joyride in an old barnstorming biplane. So he was excited too! But I think he enjoyed my excitement even more as he shared my great adventure.

We saw the red roofs of Sydney's houses. We saw fields and trees and tiny cars—and even tinier people. I felt a pressure in my ears and a strange feeling in my stomach as our shiny silver bird climbed upward to make its way to Canberra.

What a morning that was! We flew on for about an hour. Then the feeling in my ears told me that we were coming down. The ground was getting closer and closer. The tires squealed as we landed at Canberra. Back to earth again.

The War Museum was much better than I had expected. I particularly remember the Lancaster bomber and the Spitfire and the other warplanes of renown on display. Polished and clean, the objects of my awe and passion. So close I could almost touch them.

Parliament House didn't impress me much. As we looked down from the visitor's gallery it seemed to me that those politicians were just a bunch of men in church clothes shouting at one another—all at once! All I remember about the Institute of Anatomy is row upon row of jars containing pieces of pickled people!

By mid-afternoon I was fidgeting. *Let's get back in the air again,* I thought impatiently.

I couldn't appropriately express to my dad how I felt about what he had done for me—something so unbelievably wonderful. My "thank you" seemed quite inadequate. I remember taking his hand as we walked across the tarmac that evening back in Sydney. I had thought myself too old to hold my dad's hand. That was for little kids. But not on this day. This was different. This was a hand-holding day!

I sensed his deep, smiling pleasure.

What a day it had been!

But neither of us knew what a milestone it had really been in my life. A crossroad. A significant intersection.

I write this story sitting in the terminal of the crowded San Francisco Airport. A huge Japan Airlines Boeing 747 is taxiing by. It probably has four hundred people on board. Farther across the tarmac I see planes from Germany, Britain, Thailand, Hong Kong, and, of course, dozens of U.S. domestic jets.

I don't see a single DC3.

Passengers by the thousands scurry from gate to gate. Others sit bored-looking, waiting for their flight to be called. Some are using laptop computers, others, scratching away on their Palm Pilots. There are kids too. Hundreds of them—but none of them seem excited. Out on the tarmac airline employees are racing around each other in tiny tractors, some with luggage carts snaking along behind. I don't see a single fuel truck.

This isn't Mascot, and the thrill is missing. Things have changed. People seldom walk out across the tarmac to their airplanes any more. Stewardesses rarely stand in the breeze by the stairway.

I recall a lifetime of years involved in aviation. I see myself now, an aging man who has spent thousands of hours sitting in airplanes as a passenger. Then, looking back a few years, I see a much younger man flying hundreds of different airplanes, and I have a vision of piles of logbooks filled with record of almost twelve thousand hours I have flown as a pilot. Then I see a sixteen-year-old going solo for the first time, and a fourteen-year-old leaving school to work and earn enough money to fulfill his dream of learning to fly. And finally I see that wide-eyed, awestruck young boy taking his first flight in a shiny DC3.

But I see something else. Someone else. I see my dad.

I see his smile. I sense his love. I feel his pleasure. And I grasp his hand once again.

The joy comes back—and I feel a little like crying. My dad has long since gone to be in heaven with Jesus, but it feels as if he is sitting here with me, smiling again as I write his story.

And I feel the love of another Father as well. A Heavenly Father who, eons ago, planned that day for me. I feel his hand in mine too. He had things ahead for me of which I could only dream—a unique plan for my life. I had my first glimpse of it that day. That boyhood flight in an ex-military DC3 heralded a lifetime of adventure beyond my wildest dreams. My Heavenly Father gave to my earthly father the joy of sharing the moment when I first realized that my cherished dreams could become reality.

Tears come to my eyes when I think of that Heavenly Father as well. Tears of gratitude and love for what he has allowed my life to be.

It feels as if my dad is here with me today, watching the hustle and bustle of this modern airport. And so is the God of creation, the Master of the universe. I'm so glad that all my days were ordained for me. Especially that one.

How great is the love the Father has lavished on us that we should be called children of God.

1 JOHN 3:1

Chapter

3

TOO CLOSE FOR COMFORT

Death was seconds away.

My Meteor was hurtling, almost vertically, downward. The ground was racing closer and closer at a frightening rate. I didn't dare look at the airspeed indicator, but the needle must have been right up against the red arc—well in excess of 550 knots. I did see the altimeter winding down like a clock gone mad. Both throttles were closed, the air-brakes deployed, but it seemed as if the plane was still accelerating. I was pulling the control column with both hands, with all my might, back into my stomach.

God, I'm not going to make it!

There was a very slight change in attitude. The nose began to rise. But there was no change in the aircraft's direction. It was headed straight toward the ground.

No response.

In my frantic attempts to raise the nose of the aircraft, my arms and head felt like lead, my body, as if it weighed a ton. The G-force was extreme. With mouth wide open under my oxygen mask, I was groaning aloud, pleading with the aircraft to recover. It felt as if my cheeks were against my chest, my eyeballs almost popping out of their sockets.

The difference between life and death would be measured in microseconds. But the choice had been made. And there was absolutely nothing more I could do about it. I was far too low to attempt ejection. I knew death was approaching at a horrifying pace. I had heard that time seems to expand under such circumstances. It certainly did for me that day. Ironically, it seemed my thoughts were crystal clear and almost in slow motion. I recall being utterly furious with myself.

"I'll end up just like Harry," I thought, "and I can do nothing about it."

In my mind I saw again the image of a huge, irregular hole in the ground, about forty miles from my base, where a couple of months earlier Harry's Meteor had buried itself with incredible force into a farmer's field during a night exercise. A few days later, as we solemnly carried Harry's coffin at the military funeral, we all knew that the heavy weight on our shoulders was artificial. The only remains left of our friend would have fit into a shoe box.

"You fool!" was my desperate cry as that terrible dive continued. "You utterly stupid fool. Your life . . . your mission . . . all gone . . . through absolute recklessness."

I can't remember the final moments of that deadly descent or the recovery from it. I had totally blacked out. My first recollection is of the instrument panel slowly reappearing, as through a thick fog. The altimeter needle was turning clockwise now, indicating that I was climbing again. But with no power from the two engines, and the speed brakes still deployed, the airspeed was quickly deteriorating. The aircraft was on the point of stall.

I rolled the plane over to level flight, applied power to the engines, retracted the speed brakes, and ran through a checklist to ensure that all was well. Everything seemed okay. I sat, shocked, pale, and breathing heavily. I blinked my eyes, clawing my way back to full consciousness.

Somehow I had gotten through.

I nursed the jet home gently. After shut-down, I reported to the engineering officer that it had almost certainly been overstressed and would need a thorough check-up. I didn't speak to anybody in the crew room. I just signed off the flight sheet, got into my car, and drove back to my quarters. I was so ashamed of my foolishness. I found myself confessing to God how close I had come to ruining my life. I thought of my family, my parents, my siblings . . . and the anguish there would have been in our home. I castigated myself for running so perilously close to death and jeopardizing all I believed life held for me in the days and years ahead—God's plans for me.

The rest of the afternoon was spent in a somber and sober mood. The ramifications of my actions raced around my mind. Over and over again. How could I have let myself be so irresponsible?

The flight had been listed on the squadron operations sheet as "Army Co-op." I'd been doing it for the entire week. The first few runs had been fun and not overly demanding. The object of the exercise was to train young army officers to call for air support when engaged in ground battle. These simulated exercises were usually conducted on huge military reserves northwest of Sydney. I would be given coordinates to identify the general position of the army group and then fly into the area to await the radio call from their instructor. One by one, the trainees would take the microphone, identify the type of attack they wanted, the weapon required, and give the coordinates for the target.

It might be something like, "Para 35, request rocket attack on a bridge, coordinates Tango Romeo Echo One Six. Advise commencing attack." Once the target was identified, the aircraft was positioned to roll into the dive and carry out the most efficient attack possible. Pulling out of the dive would be at a prescribed height. There was no danger to anyone on the ground, nor to the aircraft—assuming minimums were adhered to.

Thus, up and down I would go. From 25,000 feet . . . down to 500 feet. 25,000 feet . . . 500 feet. Again and again. Over and over.

After a while it really became quite monotonous, which was why no one on the squadron fought to be assigned to this role. We all much preferred firing "live" weapons on a gunnery range or attempting to shoot each other down in air-to-air combat training. We even preferred the scenery of a high- or low-level cross-country flight. And this day was the last day of my weeklong assignment to army co-op. I was glad it would soon be over.

It had been on the second to last attack, while at the bottom of a dive and rather close to the ground, that I saw, for the first time, the men who were actually making these requests of me. Usually they remained undetected. But there they were. A couple of khaki-colored jeeps with long antennas and a squad of military personnel in camouflage fatigues. They were clustered together beneath some trees. I marked their position on the map.

"I'll give you some hurry-up before we're through today!" I said to myself.

At the completion of the last of the simulated attacks I climbed to 25,000 feet. The call came.

"Para 35, you're clear to base. That's all we want. Thanks. Out." This was my chance.

"Out, eh? Not likely," I muttered to myself. "You're not finished with me yet. You blokes have kept me doing this all week. Now it's my turn! And hang the 500-feet minimum!"

I rolled the aircraft onto its back, to them a tiny speck in the sky far above. Applying full throttle to gain some speed, I began my 25,000-foot, near-vertical dive. In seconds I had the jeeps in my gun sight. They loomed larger and larger as the plane screamed toward the ground.

Attack dives were never as steep as this. So my pull-out point was more a matter of guesswork than procedure. "Now! Now! Pull out now," I thought. But I was determined to give these soldiers something to remember. And the seconds ticked by. Precious seconds.

The very instant I initiated recovery from my near vertical dive, I knew. I had left it too late. I pulled back with all my might on the control column, applied the speed brakes, and slammed the throttles closed. But nothing happened. I plummeted earthward.

The Meteor, at a high dive speed, sometimes displayed a peculiar characteristic. It would change attitude but not direction. So, while the nose of the aircraft was beginning to rise, the aircraft itself was actually continuing downward, "squashing," in a screaming vertical fall.

It was utterly terrifying. Even as I write, the adrenaline flows again. And I relive the desperation of those last few seconds—before I blacked out.

———

I had no desire talk to anyone as I entered the mess that night. The army detachment was stationed at our air base. They would be dining there too. I knew that my afternoon display of bravado might just as easily have killed them as well as me. I was convinced I would be severely disciplined, perhaps even court-martialed.

Very apprehensively, I watched as the army group entered the mess later in the evening. Almost immediately, their commander asked the question loudly. "Who is Para 35 with 75 Squadron?"

I squirmed uneasily behind my newspaper. One of the pilots gestured my way.

"Meyers, are you Para 35?" the army commander asked, making his way toward my table.

"Yes, sir," I replied, putting down my paper and standing to attention. He approached my chair. I stammered. "I know what you're going to say, sir. And I—"

He motioned me with his hand to stop talking. "Son," he interrupted, "I've been in this army for many years. I've seen operations in two wars. I've called down air support in live situations on many occasions. But never in all my experience have I seen a display of precision flying like you turned on for us today! That was incredible! Absolutely amazing."

I was flabbergasted. He estimated that my aircraft was five feet from the ground, below the level of the jeeps, as it roared by! And he thought it was brilliant!

But I knew it for what it was. An escape from death by a matter of inches. I can only imagine what the soldiers would have thought had they known that this daring and most impressive display of airmanship was being carried out by a completely unconscious pilot.

After that experience my flying became somewhat more measured and, hopefully, mature. I thought about it for many, many weeks. "What if?" questions kept coming back. What if I had delayed that pull-out one more microsecond?

Would God have moved Planet Earth just that little bit off its prescribed orbit to preserve my life? Of course not. We each are charged with the responsibility to manage our own lives, to live in a disciplined way within the parameters of maturity and common sense. And I went very close to throwing my life away.

And as I think about it today, I would never have known Jo. Our five wonderful sons would never have been born. I would not have done what I have been privileged to do. My life would have been nothing more than a dim family memory by this time.

God is undoubtedly trustworthy. We can trust him for anything. He will always do his part and fulfill his promises. But we, too, are a part of the equation of life. We have a part to play. Each choice we make has its own result. It is not God whose trust is to be doubted. It is in the responsibility we have for our lives, in the choices we make, that the challenge lies.

———

The Bible records some excellent advice that Paul gave to his protégé Timothy. He said,

---

"Timothy, guard what has been entrusted to your care."

1 TIMOTHY 6:20

Good advice!

Chapter
4

BEAUTY FROM ASHES

She stood below my window, a duffel bag slung provocatively over her shoulder. "Don't you want to come with me?" she said.

I envied the lifestyle of my friends with whom I worked, and flew, every day. They were wonderful guys. I loved being with them. But they enjoyed a certain freedom that I could not experience. Not as a Christian. They could do what they liked! None of them was bound by Christian criteria of behavior. None of them had made any sort of Christian commitment. And they seemed to me to have such a great time. No restrictions. And so often, all they wanted was to include me in what they thought was fun. They didn't press. They simply offered. "Come on, man, come with us this weekend," they would say. "There'll plenty of fun. Plenty of booze. Plenty of sex." They thought they could help me enjoy life more.

It was Friday. The girl who now stood outside my window was exceptionally pretty, with a great figure and a vivacious personality. She worked as a secretary in the air-base office. My thoughts were often filled with fantasies of being with her. To my amazement, a few days before, this very girl had invited me to go away with her for the weekend. I didn't think she even knew who I was. "We're all going," she said, "all your friends, and a whole lot of girls. Why don't you come with me. We'd have a lot of fun. It'll be a wild weekend!"

I was proud of the career choice I had made. It was the fulfillment of my boyhood ambition, my driving passion. But this was a different kind of choice. It was tough. It wasn't a career choice, and yet it was absolutely crucial. It was about lifestyle. Character. Faithfulness. Discipline. It was about sex and moral integrity. And the outcome of my decision would have a profound effect on my life.

Now, I had to choose. The thought of being with this girl had consumed my days and haunted my nights. I felt distracted, confused, and very vulnerable. In my mind I argued for a compromise. I could at least experiment! Maybe I could give this attractive and tempting lifestyle a try for a while, enjoy it, and then turn my back on it! My family and Christian friends at home would never know! My world was far removed from theirs. In every way. It would be so easy. So new. So much fun.

But God would know. And I would know. So the battle raged on. And I prayed. I didn't know what else to do.

They were all getting ready to leave, and here she was, standing, waiting, invitingly. "Please come," she said again, with a dazzling, alluring smile.

How could I possibly say, "No, I don't want to"? What a liar I would be. I had to decide. I had to choose.

It was a pivotal moment. I braced myself.

"I'm sorry. I just can't come." I said.

Almost immediately the battle that had raged within me all week was over. Minutes later, as she and my squadron friends drove off, I could hardly believe that I had somehow found the guts to say no. I greatly envied them the weekend that lay before them. And yet, at the same time, I knew that I had made a good decision. The right decision. I knew that had I gone with her it would have impacted my life profoundly. I knew I would have been irrevocably changed. I would have tarnished the standards I cherished and, I believe, jeopardized my future direction.

The pressure was gone. I felt a touch of approval, a godly hand of encouragement on my shoulder, as if a heavenly messenger was saying to me, "Okay, boy, that's over. The Father says you've done well. He'll have someone special for you later. You wait and see." And I thanked God for the courage he had given me.

Such choices are tough. They require a degree of strength that is often beyond us.

But he does give the strength, even in times of inordinate weakness, to make the right choice.

———

Not a pilot in the squadron was older than twenty-five. Our commanding officer, a major in the United States Air Force, was on exchange duty with the Royal Australian Air Force. He was a great guy. But then, he could afford to be. There was no war going on.

The Meteor fighters we flew were relatively old. The F86 Avon Sabre was the attention-getter, the first RAAF aircraft capable of supersonic flight. Our squadron was slated for re-equipment with these topnotch aircraft, but until that happened we weren't really in the public eye. Our more senior pilots were working on a Sabre conversion course that left us, the newer and younger pilots, somewhat to ourselves. This only meant one thing: exhilarating, extravagant fun!

It was playtime! Especially Friday mornings.

The British would call it a *stouch*. In reality it was little more than a modern-day "flying circus." Unauthorized, but sanctioned! It took place every Friday morning at 0900 hours! There were four fighter units on our base. Two would be assigned to attack the base and two to defend it. Soon after 0800, as many as nine fighters—Meteors, Vampires, and Sabres—would depart and take their positions. They alone knew where, but some twenty to thirty minutes later, they were ready to attack. Shortly after the first wave, another similar brace of fighters would take off in time to defend. Then, without warning, it would be on.

The ensuing melee over the base, with aircraft chasing each other, rolling and turning, looping and diving, high and low, was something to behold. A glorious airborne fracas.

"Red Four, look out, there's a Sabre on your tail!—Blue section, break right, break now, now!" The air waves were filled with excited, pumped-up young voices. "This one's mine!—Gotcha!—There's a twosome, three o'clock high!—Blue Three, is he still there?—You've gone, man, you've gone, you're finished!—Where the heck did he go?—I'm on minimum fuel—I'm out of here!"

It was the chatter of battle. Playing for fun, but training for keeps!

For the ground crew, it was Friday morning entertainment!

Finally we would all land, wet with sweat and low on fuel. We had all pulled so much "G" trying with all our combined skill to shoot each other down and to avoid plowing into some unsuspecting farmer's field, we were totally exhausted. There was no live ammunition, of course, but an hour or two later when the camera gun film was shown, there were "winners and losers" nonetheless. And "kills" were proudly recorded.

Who would ever walk away from a job like that?

In 1957—at twenty-two years of age—I did.

Our squadron had been informed that when the re-equipment with Sabres was complete and we were proficient, we were to be moved to Malaya. Our new assignment was an active role in combating terrorist activity. Fooling around would be over.

There was only very scant news of terrorist incursion in Malaya. It certainly did not constitute an international threat. I recall asking a member of a bomber crew who had been in the region, "What do you attack?" He seemed to have no clear idea. It was just a matter of bombing assigned villages or jungle encampments. Another pilot said, "We try not to think about who gets killed. But as sure as night follows day, people do get killed."

Instead of being excited, as were all my fellow pilots, I began to feel a measure of disquiet. I knew I wasn't a fighter pilot just to have fun. I was not a pacifist. But the thought of being personally involved in indiscriminate bombing in peace-time, as a Christian, began to really disturb me. These feelings of discomfort grew and grew as the weeks went by. For the first time in my Air Force career I was not performing well. RAAF life began to take on a different meaning, and fighter flying lost some of its glamour. Was the door beginning to close on this chapter of my life?

And so it was with a strange mix of confidence and apprehension that I approached my commanding officer to do the unthinkable for a fighter pilot—request a change of assignment. My American CO quickly referred it on to the base commander. It was a serious matter and soon became the topic of conversation in the crew room. When the time came for me to see the base commander, I was embarrassed and nervous. I had never had a one-on-one meeting with an officer of his rank!

"What's all this about, Meyers?" he began. He listened as I struggled to explain. I endeavored to be very up-front about my position as a Christian. I was not trying in any way to be disloyal, nor was I refusing to accept an assignment. I was simply responding to deep apprehension about the task ahead. I told him about my long-term goals, my firmly held sense of calling to mission flying. I shared with him the distressing realization that I might be killing exactly the kind of people I would be serving in the years to come. To my great surprise, he was very understanding, even sympathetic.

"You've done well here, Meyers," he said. "I really respect you and admire your convictions." We talked for about an hour. Finally, he said, "I will recommend that you be transferred to the Transport Wing, to the section currently in the U.S. being trained to fly the new C130."

I was going to fly the Hercules. Another wonderful aircraft.

I was wrong.

When my reassignment papers came, I was shocked. There was no posting to the Transport Wing, no assignment to fly the C130—or any other aircraft. Instead, my posting was to Adelaide, to non-flying administrative duties.

That was the "bottom of the pack!" I could hardly believe it as I read my orders. A non-flying job! Grounded! Administrative duties! The Air Training Corps. Oh, God! Not that.

I found myself second-guessing my decision. Had I known this would happen, I would never have sought reassignment. I would have gladly stayed on as a fighter pilot. But to have my flying career cut off—was more than I could bear.

And I was deeply embarrassed in front of my fellow pilots. Grounded! I just couldn't believe it. I felt like curling up into a little ball and crying myself to sleep that night. I felt discarded, let down by the Air Force—and by God.

In the weeks before I left, every day, I would see them. Those wonderful airplanes, in precise lines, sleek and gray. I would feel their engines crackle as my friends took off, two or four at a time. "That's my life going on out there," I would think to myself. "The fulfillment of my childhood ambition. That's what I have been so good at doing . . . and I have spoiled it, ruined it." My fighter career was over. The guys I had worked with, my best friends, considered me a fool. And there was no one else to blame but myself.

Dark days.

The squadron eventually went off to Malaya with their magnificent F–86s. I went to Adelaide, with my briefcase full of administrative papers, dejected, broken-hearted.

"Where is God in all this?" I asked. "I did this for him, because I believed he wanted me to. And look at the result!"

But the pain was to worsen. I was to be accommodated at the Edinburgh Air Force Base about twenty miles north of Adelaide, where the operational unit for the multinational Weapons Research Establishment was located. From Edinburgh, highly classified and exciting test and development flying was carried out. I would be living with the men who did that flying, but every day I would have to drive twenty miles into the city—to work in an office.

Over and over again, in desperation, I cried out to God. I wondered whether he really knew what was happening. I doubt that any new appointee to a job has ever felt as negative as I did when I checked into my new responsibilities in Adelaide. I was assigned my office and sat there looking at all the "stuff" of administration—filing cabinets, typewriters, foot-high heaps of files, and orders posted on the walls. I was devastated.

Could anything be more in stark contrast to the Friday morning dogfight at my old fighter base?

There was one small consolation. The pastor from my old church in Sydney was in Adelaide now. I desperately needed a listening and sympathetic ear, a shoulder to cry on. He would understand my misery and could comfort me in my despair. At least I could go to him.

Thus, on that first afternoon, as soon as I could get away, I went to see him. It had been some years since we had met.

"What on earth are you doing here?" Alan Tinsley asked joyfully, surprised as he opened the door. "I heard you were going to Malaya." He and his wife were just the same as I remembered them; she, beautiful and elegant, warm and welcoming; he, a large, outgoing man with a soft heart and a firm handshake.

I told him everything. It all poured out. My feelings of misgivings about Malaya, right through to my arrival in Adelaide earlier that day. He listened well. He always did. But his response was not at all what I expected. I had come for comfort, consolation, and sympathy. But as my tale of woe came to an end, he looked me right in the eyes and said, "Who do you think you are? I never thought I'd see you in such a miserable state of mind, filled with self-pity. You're streets away from trusting God, Max!"

And over the next hour he delivered tough love to me. "Where is your trust in God?" he asked. "Do you think he doesn't know all about this? Do you think he has been frustrated by the Air Force in his plans for you? Come on, boy. Lift your backside off the ground and walk tall again. God knows exactly what he is doing with you. He is in complete control. Wake up to yourself—and address this thing as it really needs to be addressed."

After he had prayed for me, he said, "Now, let's go and have dinner. Joy will have something special for us. Then I'm going to send you around to the church where the choir will be rehearsing. You can sing some of your woes away!"

Sing? That was the last thing I felt like doing. "No way," I thought.

But Alan Tinsley, my friend and mentor, was a strong man. He wasn't fooling. Dinner over, Joy left for the choir practice while Alan and I chatted for a while. Then, as promised, he packed me off to the church, much against my will. It took me only a few minutes to walk the short distance, and as I entered through the vestibule I could hear the strains of a familiar anthem. Opening the door and feeling rather embarrassed, dressed as I was in my Air Force uniform, I walked right down the long aisle. The choir members, sitting in the angled seats under the pulpit, watched me all the way. I told the choirmaster that the pastor had said I was to sing in the tenor section of his choir!

It all seemed incongruous. Yes, I had always loved to sing—but not tonight! When I took my place with the tenors, I felt like crying, not singing! What a day it had been. What an emotional roller-coaster.

As we practiced familiar old anthems, however, I slowly began to feel better. A therapeutic work was being done in my heart. It was as if the arms of God were folding me to himself. The words and music we were singing were soothing my troubled soul.

I also knew that Alan Tinsley, in his home around the corner, was praying for me. His words of tough love had hurt. But Alan and Joy had always loved me like the son they never had. And the truth of what he said had broken through the gloom of my anguish.

Standing in the tenor row of the choir stalls I began glancing around. These people were strangers to me. And as I looked down into the ranks in front of me, seeing only the backs of the sopranos, my attention was drawn to a girl standing beside Joy, the pastor's wife. A mass of curly blonde hair spilled over the shoulders of a blue dress. A very nicely put together, athletic body with shapely legs and ankles that really captured my attention. My misery receded further still.

Come on, I chastised myself. *This is a house of God.* But I guess boys will be boys! And I thought, as I looked down during a pause in the practice, *The back looks really great. I wonder what the front side is like?* Then between anthems, as the next piece of music was being distributed, she turned around.

She looked at me. And I loved her. It was as simple as that. I didn't know her name. And I certainly knew nothing about her. All I knew was that she was the most exciting, spectacular girl I had ever seen in my life. Suddenly I was glad I was there. Not anywhere else. Not even getting ready to go to Malaya.

I think there was a twinkle in God's eye as he looked down on me.

After choir practice was over, people chatted and introduced themselves to me. They were so friendly, so welcoming. But I could not keep my eyes off the girl in the blue dress. The memory of her standing there by the organ on the red carpet, talking with Joy Tinsley, is one I shall never forget. Then Joy turned to me and said, "Max, I want you to meet a friend of ours, Jo Lawton." A pair of blue eyes looked into mine. "Hi, it's great to have you here. You have a really nice voice. I could hear you singing behind me." I know we talked for a few minutes, but I am sure I was utterly incoherent.

Walking out to the parking area shortly afterward, I was in a daze. And to my absolute delight, Alan, who had offered to drive me back to the Air Force base, called out to this captivating curly-headed girl, now standing with someone else, "Hey Jo, come for a ride! Joy and I are going to take this guy back to the RAAF base at Edinburgh. Come on. We'll drop you home later."

I was incredulous. Intrigued. In love. And I was going to ride with her in the Tinsley's car all the way back to the base. My misery had vanished.

I learned that this Jo Lawton was a gifted musician. For most of her twenty-three years she had played the piano. Having studied with one of Australia's great teachers and graduated from the Elder Conservatorium of Music, she was now a high school teacher of music as well as physical education. A fine organist. A choir director. I wasn't to learn until much later that her own dream, her own driving passion, had always been to one day become a missionary doctor.

At first I thought that she had been placed in my path as a further test of my commitment to serve in mission. There was no way I could imagine this girl, from such a cultured background, living in the jungle where I was planning to spend my future. But she would. She was designed for me. An incredibly intelligent, exquisite love-gift from God, she had been chosen to be my life's partner and would love me, walk with me, fly with me. She would bring to my life a great measure of richness and sophistication, enhancing and encouraging in me the development of so many qualities I would need in future years. And while I wasn't to know until much later, this Jo *was* mine. That curly-headed blonde from the soprano line eventually became my wife and the mother of our five boys, Michael, Timothy, Jonathon, Robin, and Christopher.

I didn't know, as we climbed into the back of the car that memorable night, that she would eventually leave her world, put aside her own dreams, to join mine. All I knew was that I had fallen hopelessly in love. Some months later, to my profound joy and great surprise, I found that she had fallen in love with me at the same time.

A chance meeting? Love at first sight? Or a miracle in the hand of God—a masterstroke on the canvas of our lives.

From the soprano line in the church choir that night, Jo began a flight with me that has enhanced my own flight. She has brought immeasurable strength and power to me and to many others as well along the way. She has been used in the lives of many people who serve all over the world today.

For me, this life of ours has been relatively easy. I grew up wanting to fly. That dream became my calling in teenage years, my reality as an adult. I've been involved in aviation for almost all of my working life. But for Jo it has been different. She didn't grow up with a passion for airplanes. She was highly successful in a totally different arena. Then, at twenty-three, I came into her life and it took a completely different direction. There was to be no more playing with symphony orchestras or conducting beautiful choirs. No concerts to go to, no record-player, not even a piano for a long time. Hardest of all, no dreams of a new career in medicine.

It has been a profound sacrifice.

———

I could have gone to Malaya. I certainly didn't choose to go to Adelaide. I hated the very thought of that assignment and felt dragged there like a resisting puppy. But I was being led by a Master who, although I didn't understand it, knew what was best for me and wanted me to have it.

And I have found him to be totally and completely trustworthy. It was his plan, implemented through others, that brought Jo and me together.

We were married by Alan Tinsley. We walked out of the church under the shiny crossed swords of an Air Force honor guard. Alan and Joy stood in the background, smiling.

Eventually I was assigned, as a pilot again, to Edinburgh Air Force Base, that place of so much sadness on the day of my arrival in Adelaide. The flying experience I received there in the next two years was beyond imagining in its value, far surpassing what it would have been had I remained a fighter pilot. I flew seven different types of aircraft—twin- and four-engined bombers as well as fighter and transport aircraft, even the huge Vickers Valiant, one of the three British V-Bombers. All of this was in a weapons research and development mode. In my final year I flew an aircraft for America's NASA, working to train Project Mercury tracking crews. This was an added bonus in what proved to be the best technical preparation I could possibly have had for service with MAF. A wonderful gift from God.

But God's most precious gift to me came from the soprano line in the church choir that night.

Many are the plans in a man's heart, but it is the Lord's purpose that prevails.

PROVERBS 19:21

"For I know the plans I have for you," declares the Lord, "plans to prosper you and not to harm you, plans to give you hope and a future."

JEREMIAH 29:11

Chapter

5

TOUGH DECISIONS

Flying airplanes with safety always demands maturity in decision-making. Wise choices. Military flying, I had found, was usually under close direction. Following orders. But I was to learn that MAF flying brought with it an added dimension of responsibility, choices that were often mine, and mine alone, to make. And sometimes, those choices were tough.

One evening, at about 5:30, I landed at Telefomin, a government post and mission station close to Papua New Guinea's western border. We almost never flew into Telefomin after 2:00 in the afternoon. The mountain passes and valleys in the area were usually filled with cloud by then.

But this was a medical emergency. For these flights we tried a little bit harder. I knew lives were at stake that day.

The patient was neither a Papua New Guinea national, nor mission staff. She was the wife of the patrol officer and, seven months into her pregnancy, she had gone into early labor. There were complications, however. Telefomin's small clinic was not able to provide this woman the specialist care she needed.

I had asked the staff there to have her at the airstrip. "If she's ready, I can throw my cargo off and be airborne again in just a couple of minutes. We should be able to get her to Wewak a bit after last light." It was an inhospitable country even in the daytime, so night flights were not permitted. In those days Papua New Guinea aircraft were not fitted with the appropriate instrumentation for flying after dark.

But the patient wasn't ready. She hadn't even been brought to the airstrip. "She's still down at the clinic, and has taken a turn for the worse," I was told. "We just can't move her right now."

I looked up to see the lengthening shadows beginning to darken the Telefomin valley. "Then we'll just have to wait until morning," I said reluctantly. I hoped she would make it through the night. I climbed into the waiting jeep, and we drove down through the mission station to the clinic. The valley would be enshrouded in darkness by 6:30 P.M.

But right at 6:30 there was a knock on the door of the house where I was eating supper. It was the sister from the clinic, clearly agitated. "She's in deep trouble, Max. She's getting worse and needs care that I can't give her. I don't think she'll last through the night. I've been in touch with the doctors in Wewak, but we don't have the medication they say we need. Even if we can get her to Wewak it may still be touch and go. Is there anything you can do? Is there any way that you could fly her out—now?"

Flying the airplane at night was not the problem. A great deal of my military flying had been done at night. But that was in very sophisticated aircraft, not single-engine Cessnas, and certainly not in Papua New Guinea's rugged terrain. The weather also concerned me. Conditions had been quite good as I had flown in from Wewak late in the afternoon, and the present "overcast" at Telefomin was reasonably high. But I had absolutely no idea what had happened along the track through the mountains during the couple of hours since I had come that way. The weather always changed so quickly in those mountains.

I had enough fuel on the plane to cover more than the required daytime reserves. Wewak had been alerted to the possibility of an emergency night flight and was reporting that the weather was clear. But there was no report to cover the hundred or so miles through the mountains and over the Western reaches of the Sepik Basin.

What should I do? It wasn't an easy choice. I prayed for wisdom and sound judgement. I decided to try. Before leaving I explained to the missionaries that I would need emergency lighting on the airstrip in the event that I were to find the weather impassable and elect to return. "If you hear me come back into the valley, drive one of the jeeps to each end of the airstrip. Park them just on the other side of the eastern boundary line and shine their lights toward each other. If you could also have a small fire lit at about the half-way mark on the same side of the strip, that would help."

What a place for a woman in labor, I thought as I laid her down on a thin mattress on the cold metal floor of my small Cessna. She knew only too well that planes like mine didn't fly around at night in that territory. Apprehension and fear must have compounded her pain and discomfort.

As I sat at the top end of that airstrip, my pre-takeoff checks, as usual, included a quiet but particularly earnest prayer for guidance, for help, for wise judgement. The aircraft's landing light was adequate for takeoff, but it was so dark, so very black as I climbed away toward the invisible range ahead. A turn to the right, however, allowed me to see the lights of the Telefomin station and to set a northeasterly heading between the mountains. To climb to altitude above them would have placed my patient at even more risk.

There was no moon, but I could faintly make out the rough outline of towering ridges against the night sky on either side as I flew along in the darkness. Two shades of black. Once out of the high ranges, I saw below the occasional red glow of fire from scattered Sepik villages. While still many miles from the coast, the lights of the small town of Wewak became visible, dimly at first, then a patch of twinkling brightness against the dark mass of the sea. I had lived there for years, but this was the first time I had seen the "lights of home" at night, from my airplane.

The landing at the town's airport was uneventful. An ambulance was waiting, as was the obstetrician from the hospital.

As Jo and I drove home we talked quietly. Two lives had been saved.

A tough choice. A good decision. A good result.

———

It was Sunday morning at Wasua, a Papuan village on the banks of the mighty Fly River.

We loved our little bush home there. It was a classic mission house. Perched high on wooden stilts, its walls were of plaited bamboo. It had a thatched grass roof at the front. Over the rear of the house, galvanized iron caught the rainwater and funneled it into the large tank by the back door. There was no electricity. A wood-burning stove was Jo's only cooking facility in that hot and humid environment.

Pioneer living.

Our toilet system was unique, to say the least. The "deep hole/long drop" type, generic to most mission homes, would not work in this flood-prone area. One struck water only about six inches below the surface. Instead, we had a "barely private" outdoor lean-to, containing a wooden seat positioned over a disgusting black bucket. Michael, the eldest of our five sons, now a lawyer in Australia, says he remembers as a three-year-old, that the huge spiders inhabiting the dense festoons of cobwebs in the gabled thatch of that outhouse roof were "as big as my face."

On the far side of the yard there was a large pit of sodden sawdust. In it, a veritable army of microbes and other "beasties" waited for their weekly offering from that revolting bucket. It always amazed me how clean the sawdust looked when I dug into it for the next deposit! It was like a special disappearing trick! Those microbes were masters at slight-of-hand.

Wasua really was a quaint place!

This particular morning, church was to commence in thirty minutes, and Jo was getting our three little guys ready. I walked down to the radio room to check that all was well in the network of mission stations spread over hundreds of miles from the North to the West. The people out there were "my" people. My constituency. MAF was their flying life-link.

But at Suki, about eighty miles to the west of Wasua, there was a medical emergency. "It's a snakebite case," the caller said. "We've identified the species of snake, but we have no antivenin for its poison. The man will die if we can't get him to the hospital at Daru quickly."

So much for church with my family that morning. As the congregation sat on the split-palm floor of the quaint little bush church, their harmonious Papuan singing was interrupted by the howl of the Cessna's engine as I took off along the grass airstrip about seventy-five yards away.

The flight was uneventful. The track was simple. West along the Fly River for thirty minutes, then straight ahead, paralleling another smaller river where the Fly turned up to the North. As I passed overhead, scores of crocodiles, sunning themselves on the muddy banks, slid with a splash into the water at the sound of the airplane. It was a fun place to fly. No mountains here, just thousands of square miles of tropical forest and swamplands intersected by muddy rivers, all draining into the Fly.

Finally, there ahead was Suki, and the expected group of people waiting at the parking bay of the rough airstrip. I landed and taxied to where the patient was lying on a stretcher.

He was drifting in and out of consciousness. The poison of the snake was killing him, shutting down his respiratory system by filling it with fluid. Streams of foul, thick mucus ran from his nose and mouth. Flies swarmed around his mouth, nose, and eyes. I almost retched.

In spite of his condition, he clutched firmly in his hand the head and about three inches of the body of the snake. The people knew that if they could send the offending reptile with the patient, the correct antivenin could be identified and used to neutralize the effect of the poison.

There was no time to be lost. It was a quick turnaround.

As I taxied the aircraft to the far end of the airstrip I glanced at the patient lying on the floor beside me. He looked horrible. This ghastly stuff just seemed to keep pouring from him. The nurse at Suki had thoughtfully wrapped cloth around his neck and placed it under his head to save making a mess in the plane.

I thought he was going to die—in my plane—even before we were airborne.

I prayed before I took off. For him, for healing. For me to be used in that healing process. I wondered if he would be better sitting upright. Perhaps he would be more able to breathe in that position, I thought. But there was no seat for him. Anticipating a stretcher patient, all the passenger seats had been removed and left behind at Wasua. But he could at least sit on the floor propped up against the rear of the cabin. So I stopped at the end of the airstrip, shut down the engine, and jumped out. I ran around the plane to the passenger door, climbed in and hoisted my semiconscious passenger into a sitting position, then dragged him to the back. There was no seat strap there, so he sat unrestrained, leaning against the bulkhead. The same revolting mess continued to run down his chest.

Obviously wondering why I had done this, the Suki staff ran along the strip toward me. But I didn't have time to wait for them. This man was close to death. It would take an hour to get to Daru—and every second counted.

"What's up? Why did you shut down?" one of the men shouted as he ran up to the aircraft. "It's okay," I yelled, climbing back into the pilot's seat. "I just had to change the patient's position. I'm ready now. Stand clear. I really need to get going." And with a twist of the ignition key, the engine once again burst into life. I turned into the wind and took off.

Throughout the flight to Daru, moans, horrible spasmodic coughs and choking noises continued from behind me.

There was no means to communicate ahead my impending arrival at Daru. Such a small place didn't merit a control tower. But I had a procedure worked out with the medical officer there. If I had need of an ambulance I would gun the engine once, that is, close and open the throttle, as I flew over the hospital and his house. If there was some degree of emergency I would do so twice. For a really urgent emergency, three times.

I knew he would be in church at the time, so it was over the hospital, over the doctor's house, then low over the church. I gunned the engine four, five, six times. Every inhabitant of the tiny island town would know this was an emergency!

Normally, I could depend upon seeing the dust of the ambulance approaching along the road as I shut down the engine. This time, however, I waited and waited. And I prayed, "Lord God. Please. Save this man's life."

By now my passenger was unconscious. Hoping to save precious minutes and perhaps his life, I dragged him out of the plane and tried to sit him up on the grass against the airplane's wheel. He tipped over sideways. So I propped him up again. Once more he toppled over. After one more fruitless attempt, I laid him down on the grass in the shade of the wing. "You'll just have to lie down there," I muttered to myself. He was oblivious to this strange sit-up-lie-down performance. Apart from occasional spasmodic gasps and that dreadful choking sound, he was barely breathing. I could do no more for him. Time went by. I expected him to die at any moment.

But he held fast to the snake's head.

I was thinking about getting airborne again to fly once more over the town just as the doctor arrived. Then an ambulance. "Man, I'm sorry we're late," he said as his driver backed the ambulance up to where the patient was lying. "My team must have been all over the island. What have you got for us this time?"

"Look in his hand," I said.

He leaned down and pried the snake from the patient's firm grip. "That's an unusual one. It's very poisonous," he said. "It's a rare, 'small-eyed' snake. Look." He turned the snake over. It didn't seem to have any eyes at all.

"We do have the right stuff for him," he said confidently. "I think we can save him."

The ambulance raced off with the patient on board.

I walked with the doctor to his car.

"I don't know how it is that you MAF guys seem to know so much about medical things," he said casually. "So much about everything, it seems. It's amazing. I mean, how did you know to lay that fellow down flat like you did? Instead of sitting him up."

I shifted uneasily. "Huh?" I said.

"Laying him down in the plane and on the ground here probably saved his life," he said. "Do you know what, Max? If he'd been sitting up, he would have died!"

I said nothing.

As I took off later, I thought about the ghastly coughing and choking noises. Between the snake and I, that poor man just about used up every chance he had.

The next week I flew him back to Suki, totally recovered. He sat up all the way. Again.

A bad decision. A good result.

———

I was pushing the weather in the late afternoon, trying to get back to Wapenamanda, my highland base. Having already been away for three days doing maintenance on the airplane, I tried just a little bit harder. Nights away weren't the favorite part of MAF life for Jo and me. It was much later than I would normally choose to do this flight, but at least it was worth the try.

As I approached the Central Range climbing through thirteen thousand feet to get above the rapidly rising clouds, Jo called on the radio to tell me that there was a medical situation at Kandep, about twenty minutes flying from Wapenamanda. "They're asking that you uplift a pregnant European missionary to the hospital here. It's really urgent. She's some weeks early but has gone into labor," Jo said. "They've got to get her out of there."

"Not another one of these," I thought. "Just like Telefomin." But unlike that situation some time earlier, the weather on this day was ominous and getting worse. I couldn't see how I could even get to Kandep, let alone pick up a patient and fly her back to Wapenamanda. A wall of blackening cloud and a massive range of mountains blocked the path.

However, with difficulty and by diverting a few miles, I was able to descend into the western side of the Kandep valley some thirty minutes later and carefully make my way under the low, threatening cloud to the airstrip.

A mission nurse was waiting for me. "I think we'll have to call it off, Max," she said. "She's in the final stage of labor, and she simply doesn't want to fight weather like this in your airplane. She's had a normal pregnancy thus far and, as a nurse herself, feels that the baby will be okay. Maybe she's right."

I decided to stay the night there. "There may be need for a flight first thing in the morning," I told her. "I don't think I could get back to Wapenamanda now, anyway."

The baby was born at about 8:00 P.M. Premature, but normal and healthy. There was great rejoicing.

But within minutes things had changed. The placenta had not come away, and the woman had begun to hemorrhage. Although there was no doctor present, the three experienced nursing sisters knew what to do. But to no avail. The retained placenta would not budge. And the bleeding would not stop.

By radio we made contact with the gynecologist in the regional center at Mount Hagen. His shouted instructions came through speakers set up in the bedroom. But nothing helped. Surgical intervention was out of the question. There were no facilities for typing and transfusing blood.

"If you could get her to the Wapenamanda hospital they could remove the placenta and transfuse her," the Mount Hagen doctor said during a conversation at about 9:30 P.M.

Everybody looked at me.

Another night flight? This one would not be to a coastal town like Wewak, but through ranges of high mountains to make a landing at Wapenamanda, 6500 feet above sea level, at the narrow end of a steep valley. In the dark. It was a very different challenge.

"I'll take the vehicle and go up to the airstrip," I said. "I'll look at the sky. I'll check the fuel, and I'll come back and tell you what I think we should do."

I sat in the darkness, alone, on the wing of the plane checking the fuel contents. There was no double reserve this time. In fact, I had used up some of my reserve fuel getting to Kandep and hadn't left Wewak expecting a medical emergency. If I was unable to get to Wapenamanda I would not have enough left to fly the extra seventy-five minutes on to Madang, the nearest coastal town.

"Please give me wisdom, Father," I prayed. In my imagination I could hear the cry of a healthy baby and the pleas of a frightened mother, begging. "Help me. Help me."

Opening my eyes after praying, I looked around the full 360 degrees of the horizon. It was completely dark. But in every quadrant of the sky, in turn, sometimes concurrently and sometimes very close, there were flashes of lightning. Storms enveloped the entire area. Everywhere.

It was an unmistakable answer to my prayer. But it was painful. Very painful. With a heavy heart I drove back to the mission house and told them. It simply couldn't be done. It was not possible to fly through mountainous country, with severe storms, in a fragile airplane in the blackness of that night. To do so would result in three certain deaths and the destruction of an airplane.

In the middle of the night the mother died. We sat in the house, exhausted and overwhelmed with grief.

The only sound was the crying of a little baby girl.

Next morning, as soon as the rain stopped and the clouds lifted enough to fly, I went in search of her husband. He had been on trek, visiting people many miles away to the southwest. From village to village I flew, low over the houses, until I located him traveling along a dusty track on his motorcycle.

He waved excitedly, wondering, of course, why I was flying around and around above him.

That morning we had prepared a small package with a note explaining what had happened. Having attracted his attention, I opened my window and dropped the package, with a streamer attached, into the slipstream. From above I saw him retrieve it and watched as he read it. I can see him still, just standing there, unmoving.

There was no wave as I turned and flew off back to Kandep. A good decision. A tragic result.

—·—

Some weeks later I received in the mail a large parcel from the New Zealand headquarters of the mission of my friends at Kandep. It was a magnificent coffee-table book filled with wonderful photos of their picturesque homeland.

On the flyleaf, the mission leader had written, "To our dear friend and fellow servant, Max Meyers. One who makes good decisions."

—·—

To ask for wisdom in making decisions is the right of every believer.

If any of you lacks wisdom, he should ask of God, who gives generously to all without finding fault, and it will be given to him. But when he asks, he must believe and not doubt.

JAMES 1:5–6

Chapter

6

MIRACLES AND MONSTERS

Before the airplane taxied to a stop, the smell was obvious. And for the mob of young New Guinean kids who always chased our planes as we taxied in, it was a new and pungent odor.

"This is going to be interesting," I chuckled to myself as I undid my shoulder harness and stepped down to the ground.

Crowding around the airplane, the children were soon joined by excited highland men and women, pushing and shoving, craning their necks to catch a glimpse of the amazing thing I had dragged from inside the cabin and now held suspended from my hand. Their yells and shouts of excitement drew more onlookers from the nearby government patrol post. Soon the little yellow airplane was engulfed in a mass of brown, jostling, shouting people, wide-eyed with amazement. Their excited questions tumbled out one upon the other.

"Wanem dispela samting? Wanem kain abus? Mipela no lukim dispela bipo. Em I save kaikai man?" ("What is this? What kind of creature? We've never seen anything like this before. Is it dangerous? Does it bite?")

It was only a fish.

But what a fish! Three feet of plump, sleek, silver barramundi. And it sure felt heavy, as with one hand I held it up by the gills for all to see. I had estimated its weight at probably thirty pounds. There was no scale to check it, and I had hoped that my calculations were correct as I loaded more than twenty similar fish into my Cessna 180 for the hour's flight from Lake Murray to the highlands.

To make the most of the impact, I unloaded the largest fish first. And as I took the others one by one from the airplane, the gasps of astonishment increased. The pile of inert torpedo-shaped bodies, glistening in the sun, grew bigger. I pretended to throw one to a man at the front of the crowd. He fell back on the others behind him with a yell of fear. And they all came tumbling after! Much was the laughter at his embarrassment. Looking at something so totally foreign was one thing. Touching it was another thing altogether.

These were slippery, shiny creatures—with huge, glassy, staring open eyes. No legs, no feet, no arms, no hands, no fur or feathers or hair. Interesting, even intriguing. But the unknown brings caution; the unfamiliar, fear. So the people were wary about getting too close. They wanted to see, but only the brave would risk touching these strange, exotic, weird-smelling things.

Pigs, they knew. Pigs were treasured among the tribes people of this land. They meant wealth! Birds they knew as well. Some birds were hunted for food, others for their rich and brilliantly colored feathers. Special three-pronged arrows were made for the killing of birds. Cassowaries they knew. Cassowaries were a prized, but somewhat rare, source of food.

"Wanem dispela samting?"

I tried to explain to them that these things called "fish" lived in water. Not in the fast-running, white-water mountain streams familiar to them, but in large lakes and in deep, slow-moving rivers. Any creatures living in their cold, swift creeks and rivers were very small—nothing like these huge fish. I also told them that they made excellent food.

The concept of the vastness of the ocean was beyond my ability to describe and theirs to understand. So I didn't even try.

The mission and government staff, of course, knew what I had brought. They were even more excited. Not in their wildest dreams had they ever expected to see huge fresh fish like these in their remote mountain station.

Thus, being a "fish merchant" was added to the already long list of roles I filled in my work as an MAF pilot.

———

Keith Dennis was a New Zealander who had lived in Papua since 1940 and had helped establish the work of his mission— then the Unevangelized Fields Mission (UFM), now Pioneers— at two different places along the mighty Fly River. He was one of those incredibly practical people who could turn his hand to anything. With the threat of the advancing Japanese army during World War II, he and the other missionaries in Papua New Guinea, were forced to evacuate to safety. Keith had made the long river journey to the mission headquarters at Wasua and then on to New Zealand via Thursday Island at the tip of Cape York Peninsula, the northernmost point of Australia.

Returning at the end of the war he married his sweetheart, Lillian, and in 1948 they chose to serve among the people of the remote Lake Murray area, close to the border of what was to be later called Irian Jaya. They built a large, comfortable home and mission station from local bush material at Pangoa, a picturesque headland on the Eastern shore of the lake.

"Dennis's Place" was to become a unique haven of hospitality.

Keith and Lillian had little or no contact with any Westerners in those early days. They saw their colleagues only at the annual conference of UFM. For many years the mission boat, the "M.V. Maino," provided their only link to the outside world. It plied the long Fly River from Wasua, a tiny place near the river's mouth. To reach Pangoa, the *Maino* had to leave the Fly and sail for many miles up the Strickland, then the Herbert River and into Lake Murray.

The boat brought a variety of cargo for the Dennises. Building, medical, and educational supplies sustained their work. Packaged or canned food supplemented what they grew or traded with the local people. Yet Lillian always welcomed guests, even though on occasions the menu might consist of sago, taro, and crocodile meat! The Dennises knew how to live simply; they learned from the people at Lake Murray and adopted many of their ways.

But strangely, while their home was by a truly splendid tropical lake more than thirty miles in length, they had no fish.

No fish, in a lake like this?

Keith Dennis had been a keen fisherman in New Zealand and had eagerly anticipated the excitement and fun of fishing in Lake Murray. Fresh fish would wonderfully augment their somewhat restricted diet.

He often saw tiny fingerlings and schools of small, pointed-nose garfish in the shallow waters. *Where there are small ones, there must be large ones*, he thought. But apart from the occasional almost-inedible catfish, he caught nothing.

He fished the lake from one end to the other. He tried numerous types of gear, lines, traps, bait—all to no avail. He was mystified. The people of the area hunted crocodiles and considered them a wonderful delicacy. They also had pigs—but no fish.

Passed down from generation to generation, however, were stories of huge creatures that lived in the lake. They had even been caught on occasion by their ancestors. Over the years the talk had escalated into what was a veritable legend.

A Papuan Loch Ness Monster?

But while the stories of these creatures were related with great seriousness around the village fires at night, like the Loch Ness Monster, this monster was nowhere to be seen.

There were just no fish there, no fish to be caught.

———

MAF began service to the people of the Western district late in the fifties—and changed their lives!

Wherever possible, airstrips were built adjacent to every mission and government station in the region. But not at Pangoa. Not adjacent, that is. The only place in the vicinity where an airstrip could be constructed was on the other side of the lake. And while the canoe journey was an extra chore, it still meant that the airplane did away with isolation. Instead of a number of days of boat travel along a river in hot and extremely humid conditions with a large diesel engine pounding away interminably, the Dennises could be at their mission head-quarters in a single hour of air travel. An hour of cool, comfortable flight. No more the interminable river journeys, chugging past steamy jungle trailing its tresses into limpid, brown water. Now the forest canopy sped by, like growing broccoli far below, beneath the wings of a Cessna airplane.

Life was becoming easier at Lake Murray.

But still there were no fish. Until one day—in 1962!

Sitting at breakfast, looking out across the lake through the shutters of their verandah, Keith and Lillian saw a strange and unfamiliar boat making its way toward Pangoa. They knew every government vessel that plied the waters of the rivers and their lake. The boats of the crocodile hunters who visited Lake

Murray from time to time were also well known to them. And, of course, they were very familiar with the old, faithful *Maino*. The *Maino*'s coming was always a treat for them. It meant the arrival of their long-awaited, all-too-rare order of food. It meant mail. It meant much-needed medical supplies. It meant, best of all, loved friends and visitors.

But this one they did not recognize. And it wasn't sailing on past Pangoa to the government station that had been established a few years before at the top end of the lake. It was actually headed for the little bay alongside the house.

As always, the epitome of hospitality, Keith and Lillian prepared to welcome guests. By the time the visiting boat dropped anchor, Keith was there alongside to invite the travelers in. "Hi there," he shouted. "Glad to see you. Come ashore. My wife has the kettle on."

"Thanks so much. We've come on a fishing survey," the men said. "We'll be around for a week or so and are well able to live comfortably on board. But we'd be delighted to come ashore and have some tea with you."

A fishing survey! Keith almost laughed. *They won't find any fish here*, he thought. *I've fished this lake from east to west and from north to south. I've been at it now for almost twenty years, and like some Gallilean fishermen I've read about, I've caught nothing. Apart from a few not-very-tasty catfish.*

"We'll just throw our nets over right here, then we'll be there," they said. "It'll only take a few minutes."

Keith's eyes goggled when he saw their nets. These were not nets for catching fingerlings and garfish. These were six- and eight-inch, professional deep-sea gill nets. Using a small aluminum dinghy, the men soon had them strung out from the stern of the boat, close to a patch of reeds. The line of floating corks with large glass spheres at either end was a new and unique sight at Pangoa.

My little garfish friends will smile at those as they swim on through, Keith thought bemusedly, as he waited for the men to finish their work. *I could think of better ways for the government to spend its money than on this kind of wasteful exercise.* Not wanting to offend, he said nothing. Guests like these were all too rare.

Keith later told me that for the next hour or so, while he and Lillian enjoyed the unexpected company, he was chuckling inside. After all, this was Lake Murray—his lake. His fishless lake! Anything worthwhile in this lake, apart from crocodiles, was only legendary. This was not the open sea. The thought of an ocean-going trawler—for that is what this visiting boat turned out to be—was just too much of a joke.

"Thank you," the visitors said after an enjoyable time together. Keith and Lillian were wonderful hosts, with a fund of marvelous stories. "We'll come back and moor here every night we're in the area." And then to Keith they said, "Bring your canoe and we'll have a look at the nets before we set off for the government station. We need to check in with the patrol officer there."

Keith stood alone in his dugout canoe as the men positioned their dinghy to lift the heavy net. Starting at the far end, they had dragged no more than a few feet of it out of the water when, to Keith's open-mouthed amazement, there was an enormous splash, and into the aluminum dinghy fell a gigantic, thrashing fish!

It was about three feet long and weighed more than twenty pounds.

The fishermen seemed unperturbed, certainly not the least bit surprised, and kept on with their job. Soon there was another and another of these magnificent fish flapping around in the bottom of the boat.

About five yards away, standing in his small canoe, was a goggle-eyed, totally stunned, speechless New Zealander! He just could not believe what he was seeing. These fish, these incredible fish, were being caught only yards from his house! And for all those years—those frustrating, fruitless years of fishing—he had had absolutely no indication that they were there for the taking.

By the time the net was emptied, the aluminum dinghy was loaded down with hundreds of pounds of prime barramundi.

For that is what they were. These were not just grown-up garfish. These were the best of the best, served for the pleasure and delight of discriminating diners in the most expensive restaurants of Australia.

"Would you like one for supper?" the fisherman said, handing over a fine example. They had smiled as they had seen Keith's unbelieving and astonished face. "Here, why don't you take them all. We'll keep a couple for our tests. Give the rest to the people."

Always the great storyteller, Keith later told me that for weeks he was troubled by a recurring dream. "I dreamed every night that I was standing beside a huge pile of fish, as high as a multistoried building. They were the fish that I hadn't caught over all those years."

The men who came that day were scientists as well as fishermen, and they set out to determine exactly why those remarkable adult barramundi would never take a hook or lure. But it remained a mystery. Barramundi were everywhere, not only in the area around Pangoa. Lake Murray was filled with them. They are known to be a brackish water fish and usually live around the tropical coastline at the estuaries of freshwater rivers; yet, amazingly, here they were living and thriving in the totally fresh water of Lake Murray, more than a hundred and fifty miles from the coast.

More astonishingly, these fishermen-scientists also caught varieties of fish that previously had not been known to live in fresh water or even in brackish water. They caught large sea bream and even saltwater sharks in the fresh waters of Lake Murray.

The government trawler and its crew were in Lake Murray for two weeks. They recorded their finds and associated data and then departed. Keith and Lillian Dennis waved farewell from the beautiful sandy beach at Pangoa.

They were left with many happy memories. They were left with another treasure—one of the nets the fishermen had used. "It's yours, now," they were told.

And so the people in the region had an added source of protein, a great new source of food.

Soon, the aircraft of MAF provided a way of sharing the enormous advantage of this new fishing project far and wide. No more did isolated mission and government staff have to supplement jungle food with only canned food shipped upriver on the *Maino* or flown in from the coast. In the past, my colleagues and I had flown literally tons of heavy cartons of canned meat, fish, and vegetables across those swampy wastelands.

A new era had begun. And that's how I became a fish merchant.

For Keith and Lillian Dennis to put aside their busy mission work to fish and attend to the nets was out of the question. It was a time-consuming business, particularly after another long gill net was imported and permanently set on the other side of the lake close to the airstrip. So I would land early in the morning to meet a national worker, take the canoe that was there by the shore, and motor out to the net. I would have the first pick of the catch. Sometimes my order for the day would be for only a few fish that would be thrown on top of a load of cargo already on board bound for another station. On other occasions I would fill the empty airplane with fish and set off for the highlands—a giant flying sardine can! My arrival always caused great excitement.

———

But there is more to this fine fishing tale. For the Lake Murray "Loch Ness Monster" indeed revealed itself to be far more than just a myth.

How do I know this?

Because one day I caught the monster.

We were in the canoe, and the national helper and I were pulling in the net, retrieving the expected barramundi. As we worked our way along the floating corks, the net got heavier and heavier. The thought that we may have caught a crocodile was disturbing. Trapped, a crocodile would roll over and over, creating extensive tears and tangles in the net. It would have to be taken out of the water for several days to be repaired.

As we strained to drag it in, peering hard into the clear, black water to identify what had been caught, the first thing I saw was a round, staring eye, appearing to look right at me! But this was no crocodile. The eye was brown and about two inches in diameter. I had no idea what sort of monster it was as we slowly heaved it to the surface.

To our astonishment, about ten or twelve feet beyond where my companion was standing—balancing himself in the canoe and straining to keep a grip on the net—we saw a huge tail breaking the surface! Then a large fin—and the awesome, brown, immense body of a fish, the likes of which neither of us had ever seen before.

This was no grown-up garfish. It was a sawfish. Not a swordfish, with a single, clean pointed nose. But a sawfish, with a long snout from which protruded, every few inches, sharp and dangerous-looking external teeth.

Having brought him to the surface, we decided to measure him. We cut a notch in the side of the canoe where his nose "started" and another where his tail "ended." He was seventeen feet, six inches long. He had died, caught in that nylon prison. It was impossible to lift this monster into the canoe so we cut him away and let his lifeless carcass go. He must have weighed a ton. It was a record catch. And as far as I know, my Papuan friend and I still hold that record for the biggest fish ever caught in the inland waters of Papua New Guinea.

Before we cast him adrift, I hacked off his three-foot-six inch snout with an axe. My friend took it across the lake to Pangoa where, with formaldehyde from the hospital and some good Papuan sunshine, it cured quite well. It still makes a wonderful conversation piece, a unique "show and tell."

What a fish story Pangoa turned out to be! A story of unknown, hidden treasure; an incredible resource just waiting to be discovered.

———

There are many great "fishing" stories in the gospels. A net so full that it could not be dragged aboard the boat. The coin to be found in a fish's mouth that was used to pay the taxes for Jesus and the disciples. Mending nets, casting nets, catching fish. Fishing stories in abundance.

But this Pangoa story speaks to me of something quite different—of wonderful things that are all around, available to us, if only we know how to find them. This fishing tale is a reminder of the unknown and unclaimed treasures that God has provided for us, perhaps as yet undiscovered.

Often I have heard the cry, "Where is God?" Once, in Portuguese Timor, a man who had spent years on the "hippie trail," traveling from country to country, said to me, "I've tried everything the world has to offer. I've been everywhere, just wandering. But I think now that what I've been doing these past years is, really, looking for God—but I don't know where to find him."

Like the fish in "fishless" Lake Murray, God is there. He always has been. Greater and more awesome than we could ever imagine. He is available for all who need him. Spiritual resources are there, all around us. They are there for the taking. But so many people don't even know they exist or simply do not experience for themselves the life that God offers. Many attempt in their own ways to make the most of life. They try all kinds of ways to achieve the best and be most effective. And sometimes, often, they simply give up, concluding, "This is all that life offers me. This is my plateau. This is all there is." And life becomes boringly mediocre.

And many Christians who know something of the spiritual resources that God has provided, who have "caught a few fish," still live on that plateau of mediocrity. They don't experience the abundance of the spiritual treasures freely available to them.

Yet God has more for us than we can ever imagine, "more than we can ever ask or think," he says. There is boundless joy, absolute peace, fulfillment, and richness of life—there for the asking, there for the finding.

Have you become accustomed to less than the best?

Maybe you should try another method of fishing!

Have you tried lately?

Chapter

7

FUN

Yes, there are fish in the lake at Pangoa. Along with other things.

———

With the advent of MAF service in the area, Pangoa became a popular spot where mission staff went for much needed rest and recuperation. Lake Murray's seemingly unending shoreline of tropical forest and grassland, and its exotic reed-encircled islands, stood in sharp contrast to the heavy, steamy atmosphere of so many other places in the lowlands of western Papua. With miles of clear, cool water and a great beach at the mission station, Pangoa was a perfect place for a vacation! And Keith and Lillian Dennis made it more so.

Some miles to the north, at the top end of the lake, a government officer was also stationed at a patrol post. He loved to sail, so he had a beautiful, sixteen-foot racing catamaran shipped out from

England. With white, billowing sails, racing across the waves of Lake Murray, his fancy little craft must have raised a few eyebrows among the area's native inhabitants.

Quite generously, he made the catamaran available for vacationing missionaries to enjoy. The times I spent on his sleek vessel remain among the most pleasurable memories of my years in Papua. Often, when I was "overnighting" in the area, Keith Dennis and I would go sailing, sometimes well after dark. With a stiff breeze blowing and the sky ablaze with the vivid colors of a magnificent sunset, to skim along, sitting high on the one hull, well out of the water, with the guy wires singing in the wind, was pure ecstasy.

In early 1967, Jo and I took our family there for a vacation. I couldn't wait to share with them the joys of sailing on Lake Murray. On our first evening, Keith and I decided to get up really early next morning and take the three elder boys out on the "cat" before the water got too choppy. Rob, who was the youngest at that stage, was just a little tike, barely two, so Jo stayed behind with him. Also, she had been unwell for some days before we left. While we were out enjoying ourselves, she noticed that her eyes and her skin were bright yellow, the color of a canary. Hepatitis! It was no wonder she had felt so bad.

Later that morning, before she went to bed for the next three months, I carried her out to that fancy catamaran to lie on the net between the hulls so that she could have just one chance, just one, to sail. Lillian, who was a nurse, protested loudly, Jo remembers her calling out, "You guys are crazy," as we pushed off from the shore.

After all, what could be better than sailing on Lake Murray? Except, perhaps, water skiing. Now *that* would be something to try . . .

The advantage of air service for the Dennises came at a significant personal cost in terms of their time. Pangoa was a center where cargo shipped on the *Maino* was stored for later transshipment by air to outlying stations to the north and northeast. Sometimes I would stay there for a number of days, shuttling freight to these places. Keith would put aside his own teaching and construction work at Pangoa to spend many hours working at the airstrip, weighing and arranging cargo loads and helping to load the airplane.

Announcing my day's schedule on the mission radio every morning, I would give an estimated time of arrival for each airstrip. To make sure that I was not kept waiting at Pangoa, Keith would usually leave home in his outboard-powered canoe at least an hour before that ETA. Bad weather along my route, or even a mechanical fault with the airplane, would from time to time delay my arrival and sometimes even force me to cancel the flight at the last moment. That would leave Keith waiting at the airstrip. Always wanting to please and anxious not to hold up the day's flying schedule, he would sometimes wait there for half a day. But he always gave me a joyful welcome when I arrived, no matter how late I happened to be, no matter how much time he had wasted waiting.

Nevertheless, those fruitless hours, willingly given by this dear man, concerned me. Keith and Lillian had an incredibly effective ministry among the people of Lake Murray. It seemed to me that every wasted hour he spent waiting for me was an hour of service stolen from the people.

Back in Sydney, my brother Fred had always had a power boat of some kind or another. Many were my memories of fun-filled water-skiing excursions on a river or in a bay in Sydney's picturesque environs. So I decided to write to Fred and suggest to him that there was something better to do with his latest boat. He didn't hesitate, immediately writing back to say that he would donate a boat to Keith Dennis by selling his own and purchasing a more suitable one for Pangoa.

What a great day it was when the faithful old *Maino* arrived at Pangoa with a new dinghy in tow! It was a smart little thing for those days. All aluminum, with a covered bow, a curved windshield, and full steering gear. This was no dugout canoe! And what a difference it would make! Keith could now stay on the job at the Pangoa station until he heard the sound of the airplane approaching. Then he could crank up the new boat and virtually be at the airstrip by the time I had landed. That little runabout saved hours and hours of valuable time.

And of course, it was fast! And therefore a boat with all sorts of interesting potential. What's more, Lake Murray was big. Big enough for water skiing!

So the next week, when I was at Daru I sought out the resident crocodile hunter. "George," I said, "you've told me many times how helpful and friendly the Dennises are to you when you go to Pangoa. You say that they will never accept payment for the many times they have given you hospitality." He nodded agreement, and I continued. "You know how hard they work up there, and what they do for the people. I've an idea." He was already interested.

"Did you know they have a new little runabout? How about you trying to lay your hands on some water skis and some rope? About fifty yards should do the trick. You could have them flown out from Port Moresby. When I'm down here next, I'll grab them. Keith and Lillian could really have some fun! What do you reckon?"

He grinned. "No worries, mate!"

As I taxied into the parking bay at Daru the following week, leaning up against the small tin shed, Daru's "terminal building," were two shiny new water skis and a coil of nylon cord! George wasn't there. He had set out on another hunting trip. But he had been as good as his word.

That week, Lake Murray became a resort. Barramundi fishing, sailing, and water skiing. Mission life!

It didn't seem to matter that we shared the water with crocodiles, the occasional saltwater shark, and even huge sawfish. They just had to move over. When the flying schedule made it more convenient to overnight at Pangoa, rather than sit in the boat all the way across the lake to the house, I would ski there and back!

And that was only the beginning!

One day, we needed to make a rendezvous with the *Maino* in the river to the south of the lake. We were to pick up a part for a sawmill engine, which I then had to deliver to an airstrip in the north. The *Maino* was still many hours away from Pangoa, so we decided to take the dinghy down there, meet the boat, and pick up the engine part. "Why don't you ski down?" Barry Hadlow, Keith's mission colleague, said. Sounded like a good idea to me!

Barry was a crazy driver and on the way, in a series of imaginative maneuvers, did his best to dislodge me. And, just once, he succeeded. As we passed a pretty little sandy beach on one of the many islands in the lake, on the outside of the wake and in a screaming turn, I lost balance.

In typically sardonic fashion, Barry turned the boat briefly to check that I was okay and then sped off. "See you on the way back, mate!" he called. Kept buoyant by the life jacket I was wearing, I floated in the deep water, hoping as the minutes ticked by that he really was only kidding. Time passed. But after five minutes or so, bobbing around in the murky brown water, alone, I began to wonder. And grew a little anxious. After all, what else might there be in these waters? Were there teeth that contemplated nibbling my toes?

In time, sadistically calculated, my friend returned.

On the way back to Pangoa about an hour later we passed that same sandy beach. There, basking in the sun, was a fifteen-foot crocodile. I looked with an ashen face at the huge creature. Where, precisely, had *he* been when I was in the water?

Barry thought it was a huge joke. "There are too many fat barramundi in the water for him to worry about eating a skinny coot like you!" he said. I declined his suggestion that I ski the rest of the way back.

Late one afternoon Barry was driving the boat across to the airstrip to meet me. Keith, fifty feet behind, was skimming across the water, thoroughly enjoying Barry's attempts to dislodge him and send him headfirst into the murky, predator-inhabited depths. Crouched down at the circumference of a wide arc and traveling at great speed, a patterned wake of water flying from his skis, with a huge splash, and guffaws of laughter from Barry, Keith tumbled over and over and finally came to rest upright in the water, unhurt—but minus his teeth!

His empty mouth was wide open in horror, as both top and bottom dentures drifted lazily to the bottom of the lake. A toothless man, in such a remote place. Now, that was a challenge, even for a resourceful person like Keith.

When I arrived a short time later, I was told about this somewhat unusual dilemma. I didn't know whether to laugh or cry. It was hard to express sympathy, with Barry in the background grinning like a Cheshire cat, his own teeth still firmly encased in his gums. What were we going to do?

There was an easy solution. I was planning to go to Wewak the very next day. Keith could easily come with me and consult with the excellent dental mechanic at the Catholic mission in Wewak.

But UFM had a firm policy that staff could not travel away from their station without permission. So that evening, to save

Keith the embarrassment of announcing his problem to the entire mission community on the radio the next morning, I talked to the field director, George Sexton, and got his ready approval for Keith to make the flight. They were great friends.

George was a colorful character with a dry British sense of humor, and he was not going to let Keith off the hook quite so easily.

"Pangoa, this is Wasua" was the first call on the mission's thirty-minute radio schedule early the next morning. "What's all this about Keith needing some kind of emergency trip to Wewak today?" I can just imagine the conversation around dozens of radios that morning. "That's Mr. Sexton's voice. He's hardly ever on the radio. Must be some kind of genuine emergency at Pangoa!"

The ensuing exchange was cruel indeed. For Keith! But for all the other mission staff, spread across hundreds of miles, it was a riot!

"He needs to see the dentist there, Mr. Sexton," came Lillian's response, "and Max says it's convenient to take him today."

"Put him on the radio, Lillian. I can't believe he'd want to go all that way just for a toothache," George insisted, feigning ignorance.

"Well, . . . er . . . it's more than a toothache, Mr. Sexton."

"Put him on," insisted George. "I want to ask him about it."

So, over the radio, for all to hear, was heard the struggling voice of Keith Dennis—minus his teeth. Almost inaudibly, and trying desperately to articulate normally, came the words, "I fink you know what my problem ish, Chorge. Max shed he'd tell you about it. So, letch get dis ofer wif."

But this was too good a chance for George to make some mileage out of his friend's misfortune.

"Say again? What's the problem, Keith?"

"I need a new shet of denchers."

"A new set, Keith?" queried George. "Why on earth a new set? What happened to your old ones?"

"I losht my teeth, Chorge," was the reticent, humiliated response.

His director was relentless. "How did you lose them, Keith?" he inquired.

The listening radio audience of a hundred mission staff scattered far and wide was thoroughly enjoying the break in routine transmission. It seemed to me the whole country must have been laughing.

"Any suggestions from other stations?" George asked. This was cruel in the extreme.

Suddenly the radio was jammed with a variety of innovative ideas. The first reply came from a station a hundred and fifty miles away, somewhere in the highlands.

"Get a couple of lengths of down-pipe, Keith! Put some clear plastic over the end. You may be able to spot 'em with that."

Then the dour voice of Dick Donaldson broke the airwaves.

"Hey, Keith. Tie a piece of meat on twenty-five feet of string," he said. "Then sail slowly over the place where you fell off. You never know, they might snap at that!"

In my imagination, I could almost hear the echoes of laughter from all over the country.

One by one, provocative solutions were delivered. There was no option for Keith but to endure the humiliation. That day, he flew with me to Wewak. Two days later we returned, Keith sporting a flashing new smile and an entirely recrafted reputation!

People sometimes think the Christian life is dull.

I remember a renowned English preacher who, on concluding a summer teaching commitment at our church in Australia, said as his final word to us, "This time tomorrow I'll be on my way back to England. I've had a great time with you. As I go, let this be the word I leave you with: I commend to you the life of faith, the life of following Jesus. It is so much fun!"

There is much joy—full joy—and fun in following Jesus.

———

Sharks, sawfish, crocodile—all manner of teeth lurk in the depths of Lake Murray.

Chapter 8

PERFECT PITCH

Was that a piano?

I couldn't believe it! Not here. Not on Daru.

It was unceremoniously lying on its side, on top of a heap of junk on the back of a garbage truck. Decrepit and geriatric, this was obviously its last hurrah.

But it was a piano nevertheless.

I was standing by the town jetty, speaking with the district commissioner about some flights he had requested. It was 1963. Daru was a frontier town on an island off the coast of Western Papua. It was the district's administrative and trading center. Jo and I lived just sixty miles away at Wasua, a peaceful mission station on the Fly River. There was no other airplane based in the entire area, so MAF willingly made its service available to the government as well as to the mission.

"Surely that isn't a piano," I said incredulously as the truck rumbled by.

"Yep . . . sure is. Only one in town; 'fact, only one in the western district."

"Where'd it come from?" I asked.

"Don't know," he shrugged. "Been here since before the war. In the bar at the club. Had a fair dinkum hammering in all those years, I expect. Given up the ghost now, though. Had it. Totally stuffed."

I raced over to the road and hailed the Papuan truck driver.

"Hey! Hang on a minute," I yelled. The truck rolled to a stop.

"Wait here a second, mate," I said. I ran back to the commissioner.

"Can I have it?" I panted. "Don't dump it. It's a piano! My wife would kill for a piano."

"Max! It's rotten inside!" the commissioner said. "Termites have eaten away the board that holds all the wires. It's finished, man. It's junk!"

"I don't care!" I said. "Its condition doesn't matter! We might be able to make it work. Maybe it's redeemable! You can put it on the next boat going up the Fly! They can drop it off at Wasua for me!"

He shook his head. He clearly thought I was a nut. But he had the authority to let me have it. He walked over and reluctantly told the truck driver to take the old relic to the government store rather than to the dump.

And it was that simple. We now owned a piano! A second one, in fact.

We had been living in Papua New Guinea for two years, most of the time in Wewak on the north coast. There was only one piano in the town, so a year after our arrival, although we realized that it would probably end its days there, we decided that we would ship Jo's piano from Australia. Life was not really life without a piano. Hers had been a wedding gift from her Gran.

What a day it had been when our "first" piano had arrived in late 1962. In those days, there was no wharf at Wewak, and the ship, which came every six weeks from Australia to supply the town, was unable to dock. So an ex-World War II landing barge, owned by the town stevedore, would chug out to where the ship anchored about a half-mile off the coast. The Wewak cargo was lowered into the barge using huge, heavy rope nets. This vessel was something to behold. Its dark orange coat was not the result of a fine paint job. It simply bore the color of the rust that threatened to consume it. How it stayed afloat was a mystery.

The arrival of the supply ship was always an event. It brought frozen meat, fruit, vegetables, and all kinds of goods to restock the trade stores. Very occasionally it even brought ice cream, the most prized delicacy of all. Only the early birds were able to buy that particular luxury. It lasted a day. Most of the town went down to the beach to witness the unloading procedure. The children would leap into the sea and swim out to where the ships were anchored in the deep bay. You could hear them from the shore all day, laughing and splashing and yelling at the merchant seamen. As the years went by, our four older boys inevitably joined them. They can still tread water for hours.

Jo was down there the entire day when her piano finally arrived. She would have been out on the barge to supervise, had she been allowed, but those rough-and-ready stevedores wouldn't have her on that leaky old barge. So she waited, staring impatiently from the beach, as load after load of the town's cargo made the perilous journey to the shore. Then, at the end of the day—it was piano time.

From a distance, across the water, we watched with bated breath as the treasured crate gradually emerged, cocooned in rope, to dangle high above the hold. Slowly it was lowered into the rusty open relic. Miracle of miracles, it was neither dropped into the sea (as was the fate of many pieces of freight) nor even damaged. Carefully, we drove it home on MAF's old blue truck and lovingly removed the piano from its wooden box. It was just as she remembered it.

Jo spent the next day tuning it. How she reveled in that piano! For three weeks.

Then we were unexpectedly reassigned to Wasua. We couldn't get it there on a DC3. The airstrip was way too short. So she left her beloved piano in Wewak.

Eventually it was flown to the highlands, where Christian Radio Missionary Fellowship used it for many years in their school of the air. Every now and then we'd tune in and hear Gran's piano crackling over the airwaves.

But now we had another piano!

Unlike Gran's grand instrument, this was not an elegant piece of furniture. Sitting atop the dump truck, it looked decidedly forlorn. Once perfectly lacquered, its wood surface was now laced with thousands of tiny cracks. The lid bore a strange tattoo of small round white circles, where countless wet beer glasses had left their mark. I didn't dare to look inside.

"You wait till the next boat comes. I've got something fantastic on it for you!" I announced to Jo when I arrived home. And a week or two later our second piano, in all its glory, was delivered. This time Jo simply stood there, incredulous.

There were peals of laughter from the gathered crowd as twenty of the village men hauled the old instrument up the steep, slippery riverbank. It was placed on a wooden sled behind the mission tractor and dragged the few hundred yards along the airstrip to our house. Then it was manhandled up the lengthy flight of stairs to our open verandah. They didn't seem to exercise a great deal of care.

"Now, let's look inside," Jo said, and gingerly levered back the lid.

Clearly, Papuan termites had rarely tasted fine German timber. For there they were, happily feasting still.

Originally, all 199 pins had been set into a solid wooden plank. But now it looked more like honeycomb than wood. It had been "aerated" by thousands of hungry creatures. It was paper thin, and had long since shed most of the pins into which the strings had been fitted. Below, in the bowels of this amazing instrument, was a mess of entwined wires, looking remarkably similar to the entanglements that surround a military foxhole.

Amazingly, the dowels and felt-tipped hammers were in reasonable shape. And while many of the keys had parted with their ivory covers, they too were quite good. I guess the termites hadn't gotten around to them yet. They were enjoying the plank too much.

As we closed the lid, we looked at each other. "We have one heck of challenge to make this thing even look good, let alone play!" she commented bemusedly.

But this was Wasua! There was no television. No entertainment. We had plenty of time!

So we set about this "evening restoration" project with romantic vigor.

The first thing we needed was a new plank. Large trees were plentiful in the forests around Lake Murray, with hardwoods, softwoods, and fine, exotic tropical timbers. And there was a sawmill at Pangoa, where our friend Keith Dennis lived. Following my precise measurements, he selected a beautiful piece of hardwood that had been drying under his house for three years. He ran it through his saw, cut it to exact size, and soon had the surface shining. I flew it back to Wasua on the backload of a cargo flight.

Jo already had her piano-tuning equipment with her, and so the job began!

A thousand little white creatures decided with alacrity to depart the scene as I squirted insecticide over the honeycomb plank and shut the lid down tight. The fact that they probably marched immediately into the bush-timbers of our home didn't really matter to us. There were plenty of "locals" there anyway. Perhaps the ensuing battle would lower the population already working on the house!

The plank wasn't at all heavy when I unbolted it and gingerly lifted it out of the frame a few days later. It weighed about a pound and a half and was as fragile as a wafer. But it had to be used as a template to position the 199 holes in the new plank. This one weighed about a hundred pounds! As we disassembled our magnificent instrument, we organized all the pieces in cardboard cartons on the floor.

The internal organs of a piano are something to behold when all laid in rows. There were exquisite little dowels of different lengths and diameters, as well as keys, hammers, leather joints, tiny little pins, pieces of felt, and pieces of metal. And then there were wires, miles of them, twisted and rusty, all in a heap. It was amazing! And thoroughly daunting.

The mission at Wasua had only an old, twelve-watt diesel generator that pounded, wheezed, and gasped for a few hours every evening to provide enough electricity to run a few lights. The use of even a power drill was out of the question. So the preparation of the plank was a long and demanding job. Not only did we need to ensure that all 199 holes were correctly drilled, they could not be a fraction wider in diameter than was required. Each had to be straight and absolutely vertical. I'm sure I turned the handle of my drill a million times.

Each threaded pin then had to be carefully inserted to ensure that when wire was attached and the tuning process underway, the pin would slowly wind its way into the wood.

Finally, when we bolted the plank into the frame—it fit! And it looked great!

Next came the demanding task of sorting out the strings. Each one had to find its correct place in the fixture at the bottom and the adjustable pin at the top. The thick bass strings were more easily positioned. The finer wires of the upper register were the greater challenge, especially as they overlaid each other in groups.

And so this gargantuan task proceeded. From the Wasua village there was a constant rotation of spectators. Not being able to produce a sound yet, this unusual brown box was still a mystery to them. The fact that the pilot and his wife were working so hard on a great mess of strange things must have been the source of hours of conversation around the fires at night. Word spread to surrounding villages, and from time to time unfamiliar faces peered over the verandah. I suppose it was worth paddling a canoe a few miles or walking a day or so through the jungle to see this weird ritual.

Hour after hour, week after week, piece by piece, we labored on. At one point we joked about whether our furlough, planned for the next year, would have to be put off. But finally it began to take shape again, as a piano. The plank was firmly in place, as were the pins, the strings, the keys, and the hammer mechanism.

And at the end, amazingly, there were no parts left over!

Now, for the tuning! Out came the chromed tuning hammer and paps wedges. One by one, I began to turn the pins. Slowly the wires tightened. First a center string, then a bass string, then a treble, and so on, in rotation, so that uniform tension was applied the entire length of the plank. Night after night it continued, half-turn by half-turn. All 199 strings grew more taut by the day.

This was the tedious part of the project. I was sorely tempted to double the pace at which I was tightening them. But we didn't think that would be wise. It was becoming clear that the tension on the plank was going to be enormous. In fact, the total weight to which we were so blithely subjecting our tropical hardwood plank would be in excess of twenty tons. We didn't know this, however, and what we lacked in mathematical acumen, we were soon to discover in a memorable and dramatic way.

After a week or so of this, our piano could just about make a recognizable sound! The villagers were amazed. "Ah-ha, ah-ha," they said to each other, with nods of new understanding. Now they knew! There were smiles all round.

Jo, who was pregnant with Jonathon, was badly in need of a break. So she, Timothy, and Michael went to Pangoa for a week of rest. This was my opportunity! I would surprise her! I would have this beast singing like a Steinway by the time she returned! So on a day when rain put a stop to my flying, out came the tuning fork.

I recalled Jo cracking it against the rail of the verandah wall and holding it up to her ear to get the primary tone . . . A 440. With a flourish, I did the same and then struck the piano's "A" key to see how the two notes compared. They were not even close! I checked to make sure I had played the right note . . . the white one north of the two black ones, in the group of three. Yes. Definitely the A.

Bummer!

So I set to work again, cranking up all the strings to what I presumed to be their correct tension and pitch.

When Jo returned, it was finished . . . I thought! With pride, I called her out to the verandah. "Hey, Jo! Now! Just listen to this!"

I sat down and played her the one piece in my own somewhat limited repertoire, "Who Can Cheer the Soul like Jesus." In A-flat. I finished with a flourish, and turned to her triumphantly.

"Great, eh?"

But her face said it all.

"I can't play that!" she exclaimed, horrified. "It sounds awful. And it's an octave too low! I'll have to sit a foot to the right!"

I couldn't believe it! It sounded just fine to me. Although I must admit, "Who Can Cheer the Soul . . ." had sounded a little melancholy. I argued, but in vain. I don't have perfect pitch, like Jo.

It was back to work again, cranking and twisting on those already stressed-out wires. I winced with every turn, wondering about the strength of Keith Dennis's plank. But we were getting closer. There was joyful anticipation of the days ahead, and a house filled with music again.

Just a few more turns . . . just one or two . . . . almost right . . . the days passed.

One evening, having just about reached our acoustic goal, we went off to bed.

It was a classic Wasua night—still and quiet. Often on serene evenings like that, we would lie there and ask each other, "Can you hear anything?" The tiniest sound was discernable; an insect in the long grass on the other side of the airstrip, a dog's bark from the far end of the nearby village, a solitary cricket. Often, as on this evening, there was total silence.

Hours later, it happened.

"What ever was that?" Jo asked, sitting up. I awoke with a start.

"What ever was what?" I said. "Go to sleep. It's late."

"Shh! Listen!" she said.

I strained to hear. From the direction of the verandah emanated a most unusual, groaning creak. It was rather like the sound one might have heard on an old sailing ship. There it was again!

I too sat up.

Again!

"Ccrrrrkkkk. Crrrrkkkk"—louder and louder.

And then, all of a sudden, there was a horrendous "crack." An explosion that split the night.

We leapt out of bed. The kids woke up crying. The village dogs began to bark.

Within seconds the house was filled with a cacophony of weird, almost musical reverberations.

"Oh no!" we shouted together. "Not our piano!"

We grabbed the flashlight, ran to the verandah, and shone the beam in its direction.

The piano looked normal. It was in the same place. It appeared intact.

Where had that incredible noise come from?

We approached it slowly.

"Max," Jo whispered. "Be careful! Maybe something's trapped in there!" We often had visitors from the jungle take up refuge in our home. Cautiously I opened the lid and peered inside.

There they were. Many of them still moving, unwinding like worms in a box. And the dying strains of some surreal sonata emanated from its destroyed bowels.

I had seen this before. Months before. There was the familiar mess of wires, back again, lying haphazardly over the hammer mechanism. The piano was giving its final performance.

We watched and listened, audience to the death throes of a great old instrument.

Within minutes the Pangoa plank was split from end to end, splintered into a thousand pieces. Pointed fingers of pink wood were everywhere. Some of the pins were still firmly in place but most were lying bare, wire still attached, unwinding.

We began to laugh. All those months of work! Hundreds and hundreds of hours of loving attention. All for nothing!

Next morning, the same men who had carried it up the stairs to the verandah were co-opted once again, only this time to drop the case and its twisted contents unceremoniously over the balcony, where it smashed onto the hard ground ten feet below. Gazing down upon the heap of shattered wood, we thought about the German artisans who, so long ago, had fashioned all the pieces of doweling, the finely shaped hammers, dampers, and other delicate pieces. We imagined how lovingly they must have fitted them all together to create this fine musical instrument.

We kept a few of the strings for odd jobs around the house. It was high-quality wire. The rest we gave to the villagers. All the other metal parts were thrown away.

And the fine German timber? It had the most glorious end. We fed it, piece by piece, through the wood-burning stove in the kitchen. Day after day it yielded its remains to my trusty tomahawk—to become fuel for our cooking. Jo made many a loaf of bread with the heat it produced. What better kindling could one ever find than a hundred-year-old length of quarter-inch doweling, even if it did have a felt hammer attached to its end?

We had worked so hard at reconstructing that old instrument. We were determined to redeem it. To make it play again. But it never did. Our expectations of beautiful music were dashed to pieces, like that hardwood plank, in a single shattering instant.

And we chuckle every time we think about it.

But there is, nevertheless, wonderful music in our memories of Wasua.

Admittedly, it is not the remembered strains of an old, amateurishly-repaired German piano, but the music of laughter in the voices of those Papuan people, the harmony of their singing, and the joyful sounds of children playing underneath our house.

Yes, there were frustrated expectations of Chopin, Beethoven, and Bach. There was disappointment and a sense of wasted effort. But that is life! Someone once said that the mark of a man's maturity is his ability to cope with frustrated expectations.

But there were expectations that were gloriously fulfilled in other areas of life. We were there less than two years, but we remember it as a time of great happiness and reward as we saw the difference MAF's work made in people's lives. And we both look back with great joy to the many opportunities of personal ministry. Especially for Jo, in the lives of the women of the village.

——

By the way, God is a master craftsman. He loves to rebuild broken lives. He can untangle the twisted, rusty strings of people's lives and fit them into a new and indestructible base. He will take broken pieces and worn out keys and fashion them into a wonderful new instrument.

And ultimately, he never fails.

Paul says it well:

[For I am] confident of this, that he who began a good work in you will carry it on to completion.

PHILIPPIANS 1:6

Chapter

9

EXTREME SPORT

Question: How do you get a downed aircraft out of a riverbed deep in a remote South Pacific jungle and have it flying again in less than a week?

Answer: With great difficulty, a lot of help, and heaps of fun along the way!

There was the usual early-morning chatter on the radio. Pilots were giving departure, position, and landing reports and requesting weather and traffic updates. The flight service officers were answering questions and passing on other necessary information. It was "operations normal" on this early morning in September 1966. The day's flying was getting underway. The air was full of talk! Airplanes all over the country were feeling their way through the clearing fog and haze of a typical tropical highland day. Then—

"Mayday, Mayday, Mayday ..."

There is no other cry, no other call, that so demands instant attention and concern in the world of aviation. The response is immediate. All other communication ceases.

And so it was on this day. •

"Mayday, Mayday, Mayday, this is Bravo Victor Kilo." It was one of our MAF airplanes. "Position, Yuat Gap, over the river at nine thousand feet, descending. Total engine failure." Pilots everywhere held their breath. The call continued.

"My intention is to attempt a forced landing on the river bank at the northern end of the gap."

Land on the bank of the river in the Yuat Gap? It couldn't be done. I knew that area well. There was no riverbank there at all that could be in any way used to land an airplane. Although the river was running lower than usual, any exposed bank would be steep and muddy or a mass of huge, round rocks. You simply could not land a Cessna 185 there!

Bravo Victor Kilo (BVK) had departed from its base at Wapenamanda only twenty minutes earlier, at 7:00 A.M., bound for Wewak on the North Coast. The Yuat Gap was a familiar place, an en-route reporting point. There, the high mountains part, forming a broad canyon through which the turbulent waters of the Yuat River force their way before eventually emerging from the high country to flow on down to the lowlands.

Immediately, aircraft began diverting to the area. To everyone's astonishment, within minutes another call from Allan, the pilot. "Madang, this is Bravo Victor Kilo. Safely on the ground on the east bank of the Yuat River. The aircraft is only slightly damaged."

Safely on the ground? Only slight damage? Surely it wasn't possible.

But it was soon confirmed. Circling aircraft could see Allan waving from the rocky area where he had landed.

MAF's PNG Field Leader, Max Flavel, and I were over the site by 8:30. We could hardly believe what we saw. There, in the center of a narrow strip of large, white rocks, was BVK. The airplane appeared totally intact. Allan, as reported, was standing nearby, waving. I descended, made a tight circle just above tree level, and flew low along the river to see exactly how and where he had managed to land.

In the sunlight, framed on one side by thick jungle and on the other by the swiftly running river, the rugged little Cessna looked strangely out of place.

Soon, a full-scale rescue operation was underway. A government-chartered helicopter was already en route to the Yuat Gap. The priority was always to get the pilot out quickly. Max and I flew to the nearest airstrip at Biwat, a small Catholic mission station midway between the forced landing site and the Sepik River. We had arranged for the helicopter to take Allan there. Within minutes he arrived, having left Bravo Victor Kilo to the mercy of a rising river.

Huddled around an office table in Wewak that evening, we made our plans. We could not abandon this valuable aircraft there. It absolutely could not be lost. Its work was too important!

From Allan's report of the damage, we calculated that, apart from changing the engine, a day's work, it would only need an hour or so of repairs to make it flyable again.

But there were no heavy-lift helicopters available in Papua New Guinea at the time. Removal by river was the only way. And time was of the essence. In those parts, an exposed river bed never lasted long. One good night of rain would raise the water level, and faithful old Bravo Victor Kilo would be washed away.

The decision was made. A most extraordinary recovery mission would be attempted.

It was a full Cessna that landed back at Biwat at 0800 the following morning. Our "rescue" party consisted of Ray, an MAF mechanic, Allan, BVK's pilot, and myself. Basic food and camping supplies for a few days and a heavy airplane tool kit made up the remainder of the load.

The priest at Biwat was very helpful. He took us in his small motor launch as far as the water conditions would allow, to a riverside village called Sipisipi. It was a slow and laborious trip upriver.

Sipisipi was a most pleasant place. The people there treated us royally, unused to so many "foreign" visitors. As we drank the milk of fresh, sweet coconuts, negotiations commenced. We wanted three canoes and, we thought, about ten men. Clearly, this was no ordinary day in the life of Sipisipi. Every man, woman, and child in the village wanted to come. We eventually settled on twenty-one able-bodied men. Our village friends insisted we would need at least that many. After all, who would haul the canoes through the rapids?

Rapids? I shifted uneasily.

Two of the canoes were about forty feet in length, the other a little smaller. They sat low in the water, weighed down with food, gasoline, tools, and supplies. Barely six inches of rough wooden hull remained above the water line. It was precarious in the extreme. Gingerly, I lowered myself into my canoe. *"Sindaun. Yu noken wokabaut. Maske sanap."* ("Sit down. Don't move around. Don't stand up.") I happily obliged. There were jaws in the waters below! Hungry jaws! I had no intention of falling in. Our Sipisipi friends showed no concern whatsoever. I began to wonder whether this plan of ours was going to work. But when all was ready, our little recovery party set off.

For the remainder of that day, like intrepid explorers breaching the unknown wilderness, we crawled upriver. It was a circuitous route. The only noise was the incessant howl of three single-cylinder Archimedes outboard motors. Where in the world they came from and how they kept going remains a mystery to this day. Pieces of wire, hand-woven cord, an amazing assortment of tools, and spare parts wrapped in a dirty old cloth were on hand for any emergency. But, amazingly, those mechanical marvels ran on, howling hour after hour, their exposed little flywheels spinning crazily in the boiling sun.

As we progressed, the river became narrower and narrower—and faster and faster. In the shallower sections we could see a rough, rocky bottom. We were approaching the whitewater rapids. But by this time I had become convinced this venture might well be nothing more than a foolhardy dream. Here we were, struggling upstream in canoes that seemed barely afloat.

Soon we would be returning, *with an airplane on board!*

The procedure for negotiating the rapids was simple. Airforce pilots would call it "line astern," one canoe behind the other—with a considerable distance between them. Then, heading to the place with the least amount of "white," each driver in turn would commence the assault. Completely disregarding the welfare of his little Archimedes motor, he would plunge into the rapids at full throttle.

Inevitably, however, when there was no more headway to be made, we would await the call, *"Olgeta kalap na godaun, na supim kanu."* ("Everyone over the side and push the canoe!")

This was mountain water and very cold. But a wonderful relief from roasting in the sun.

Trying to find a foothold on the slippery rocks below was tricky enough. But manhandling a heavy wooden canoe through the rapids was difficult in the extreme. We took many a ducking, the rushing water flooding over our heads. Most of the time we just clung on, hoping that at least one or more of our crew had his feet planted firmly on the slick bottom. Then, having safely navigated an area of whitewater rapid, we would all clamber on board again, soaking wet and exhausted, and motor on to the next challenge. Sometimes it lay only a hundred yards ahead.

The day was long, laborious, and exhausting. Rapid after rapid after rapid. I clearly recall that, at one point, looking back after hours of struggling, we could still see the place where we had stopped for a break earlier that day. It was about half a mile downstream.

But what fun.

Toward evening, different shades of color in the water indicated that we were approaching the junction with another river. As we reached the mouth of the Maramuni, a river familiar to us from the air, we looked for a spot to camp. Just as the light was beginning to fade, we found a place that would do. It was not ideal, but it was all that was available. There was nothing there but jungle, water, mud, and a very small patch of somewhat level, hard clay where all twenty-four of us would be bedding down for the night.

Allan, Ray, and I were very weary. But the men from Sipisipi were still excited about this new adventure. It didn't take them long to unpack the canoes and make a fire.

Our meal of canned meat and rice was augmented by taro, sago, and bananas—the staple diet of our companions.

Before I went to sleep, I remember looking up into the black velvety sky and wondering whether the stars could possibly appear quite so bright from any other place on earth. They were like pinpricks in the floor of heaven. I marveled and worshiped the God who made it all.

I had not been asleep for more than a few minutes when I was rudely awakened. I was roughly shaken by two or three men who looked at me with staring, concerned eyes.

"Yu no ken slip. Taim yu slip, nus bilong yu em I krai. Dispela krai i olsem kry bilong puk-puk man. Sapos puk-puk meri em i harim yu, em i cam. Sapos i painim mipela, em i kross na kaikai mipela." ("We can't let you sleep. When you sleep, your nose makes a noise like the male crocodile. When the female hears that cry, she will come and, instead of finding a mate, will find us here. She will be very cross. She will eat us!")

Now, my wife Jo has never been particularly fond of my snoring. Indeed, quite the contrary. But according to my new Sipisipi friends, a female crocodile would find it irresistible.

So they took shifts to ensure that I didn't sleep all night, or at least not deeply enough to allow the sound of my gentle breathing to escalate into its inevitable raucous snore. They told me I could catch up on sleep during the next day. Sure. In a cabin cruiser! But these canoes were *not* cabin cruisers.

At sunrise the next morning I was up with the rest of them, anxious to be on our way. With Archimedes howling, we sailed off for another day of pushing and pulling, slipping and sliding, sitting and swimming, dunking and near-death experiences.

I think we were the pioneers of "extreme sport." And this was "Tarzan" country. Today people pay a small fortune to do what we were doing.

But then came an unexpected challenge. We had noticed that our Sipisipi men had become more and more subdued as the day went by. They talked quietly among themselves and called out from canoe to canoe in their own language. By mid-morning, they disclosed what was worrying them. They didn't want to go any further.

"Em i taim mipela go bek long ples. Mi ting mipela enap long painim balus pinis long hia. Mipela noken walkabaut moa." ("It's time we went back home. We thought we would have found the airplane by now. We can't go any farther than this.")

They explained that we had long since reached and passed the limits of their traditional territory. They said that our progress would have already been monitored by unknown tribespeople, fierce and warlike men who would be very unhappy that we were invading their area. They were afraid we would all be killed.

It took much talking to persuade them to change their minds. We explained that from the air we had never seen any villages further upriver than Sipisipi. And besides, we knew we weren't far from our destination. We could see hazy blue mountains ahead. In river-miles, of course, we had no idea how much farther we had to go. It was a solemn crew that reluctantly continued.

Another tiring day. On a number of occasions a propeller struck a rock, shearing off the cotter pin and sending the motor into a screeching howl. Yet again, it was into the water. While repairs were made we struggled to hang on and prevent our trusty vessel from being carried away, out of control, backward!

Finally, as evening was drawing near, our little convoy of three rounded a bend. And there it was, about a quarter of a mile ahead. Our yellow and black Cessna sat, with a certain air of dignity, on an exposed bank of huge white rocks.

Bellows of exultation reverberated up and down the river valley. We had made it!

Ray and I were absolutely astonished. In spite of its resting place, BVK was virtually undamaged. There was not even a black rubber-mark on the stones. Just a flat tire and very slight damage to the tailplane. As chief pilot, I was impressed. What an incredible landing!

Our Sipisipi companions were not so happy. Clearly nervous and agitated, they didn't want to stay. They believed there were enemy tribes all around us and, also, that there was not enough food for them to eat. We had to do something to restore their confidence, to persuade them that they would be fine. We told them it would not take long at all to dissemble the aircraft and be on the way back downriver with it.

But they were not easily convinced.

As an encouragement to them and to reassure them that we were not really at the end of the world as they feared, we called the Wewak base on our portable radio and requested that they arrange an airdrop of rice and tinned fish in the morning. The provision of this extra food supply would be advantageous as well as an incentive for our helpers to stay.

The men insisted that they mount guard on our camp that night in case of attack by marauding cannibals. Ray, Allan, and I were too weary to be concerned about such things. Obviously, I had not had my promised sleep in the canoe during the day. Thankfully, my national companions were most preoccupied. Female crocodiles were less worrisome than hungry cannibals. I slept like a log.

With the dawn came a lessening of tension. We had made it through the night without being attacked. Soon after, we heard the welcome sound of our airborne room service approaching. The Cessna from Wewak flew low overhead. The Sipisipi men were ecstatic. The right-hand door had been removed and they could clearly see the piled bags of food stacked on the door sill. Following a couple of very low runs along the river, and just at the most propitious moment, the bags were pushed out and came raining down, right on our stony beach. Nearby, BVK sat awaiting disassembly.

The airdrop worked wonders for our transport crew. They thought it was amazing. These white men had talked into a little black box late in the afternoon saying ridiculous things about fish and rice. Then, the next morning, fish and rice had come tumbling down from the heavens.

As the men had brought a shotgun with them, we had asked that a few packets of extra shotgun cartridges be included in the sacks of food. Soon our crew had someone continuously out hunting. By the time we were ready for our return trip a quantity of meat—pig, cassowary, and smaller birds—had been caught and was being smoked in a quickly made smokehouse.

The task at hand was no small feat. First, engine and wings were removed. Planning the loading of BVK in readiness for the trip downriver took quite some time. We decided to connect the two larger canoes together, somewhat like a catamaran. Then our twenty-one strong men lifted the airplane off the stones, carried it to the water's edge, and positioned it with one mainwheel toward the front of each canoe. We made a simple wooden frame between the two canoes, near the stern, for the tailwheel. It was not necessary to lash them together. They were securely held by the weight of the airplane. One wing was placed beside the fuselage. The engine and the other wing were placed in the third canoe.

This unorthodox rescue craft looked weird, to say the least, but the weight of the aircraft was evenly distributed and it seemed to ride well in the water.

Had Papua New Guinean canoes ever held such a load? I think not.

The water at our rocky beach was running fast. About five hundred yards downstream it increased in speed to become a bubbling white rapid, the first of many before becoming a smooth-flowing river. After much cogitating, we decided that until we reached those smooth waters below the area of rapids, the only way to ensure control with such a top-heavy load was to drive the canoes under power upriver against the current. Then, by reducing the throttle, we would allow the craft to drift in a slow, controlled manner downstream—backward!

We were all nervous. But the time came. It was now or never. We piled on board, taking our allocated positions, and cranked up the ever-faithful Archimedes. With the prow of each canoe headed upstream, we worked our way to the middle of the river and held our strange flotilla motionless against the current. Then, reducing the power, we began our forward-facing, backward trip home!

It worked!

The two canoes, firmly connected and now sitting lower in the water, were quite stable, providing a much more comfortable ride for us "whiteskins." We could actually sit safely on the side of the hull, and even stand up and move about.

As we approached the first rapid, more throttle was applied to counteract the increasing speed of the river. Backing, then, into the white water, the outboard motors strained to compensate for the increased current. So, as before, it was *"algeta kalap, na godaun."* Everyone over the side again, to manhandle our strange contraption, inch by inch, through the rapid to the smoother, deeper water.

Following each stretch of white water, we would rest in the calmer sections. If necessary, we baled out the canoes.

And so it went on. Rapid after rapid.

Only once did we almost lose our "ship." Perhaps the water was too deep or the rocky riverbed too slippery. I don't know. But suddenly, at one point, we found ourselves being swept away, broadside and out of control. Frantically, we grabbed onto any parts of the hull we could reach, and clung on desperately. Like a crippled bird, our wingless yellow Cessna almost became the "Yellow Submarine." It was a wild ride! We were a water-logged lot, spluttering and coughing, when finally we shot out into calmer water. Carefully we fished around and retrieved the bailing equipment, an assortment of half-coconut shells, cans, and scoops. As quickly as we dared, we emptied out the hulls before climbing back in.

As we progressed downstream, to our relief, the rapids eventually became less frequent, and we were able to return to traveling in a conventional fashion—facing forward.

Exuberant yells of triumph were shouted from the canoes as we approached Sipisipi. There were looks of open-mouthed astonishment from the people on the shore when they saw our amazing little flotilla sail past their village. We were nearly home safe!

And finally, there it was—Biwat.

Then my heart sank.

Because of the low water level, the river bank at Biwat was an almost vertical wall of slippery, terra-cotta-colored clay, about twenty feet high. It marked the airstrip threshold. I barely managed to scale it on all fours. Standing on the grass at the top, I wondered how on earth we could ever lift the airplane up to the airstrip. I began to wonder if it would be better to take our strange convoy the extra day or so downstream to the larger Sepik River, and there find an easier place to bring the plane ashore.

I shouted down to the men in pidgin.

"Listen! Please, listen."

They looked up with enthusiastic boyish grins. I barked my orders. "Do not do anything," I said. "We are not going to lose this aircraft. Not now! Not after all this effort. You are to wait where you are. We're going to have a walk around to see whether there is a way up here." I had an awful vision of the entire contraption tipping over before my eyes and the tail of BVK slipping ignominiously beneath the waters. I was determined not to allow this precious airplane to end up at the bottom of the river.

But our Sipisipi friends had other ideas.

In Papua New Guinea there are many strange sounds. But there is no mistaking the sound of a group of men at work. The only way I can describe it is as a series of great, rhythmic, corporate grunts. It is the product of enormous joint effort. And while Ray, Allan, and I were walking along the airstrip, to my horror we heard it. We turned. There, like a golden Phoenix, from the kunai grass at the end of the airstrip, rose Bravo Victor Kilo.

Incredibly, the men of Sipisipi had simply walked up that almost perpendicular, slippery wall with an airplane on their shoulders! And deposited it on the ground at Biwat.

All done. Their job was finished!

To this day I have absolutely no idea how they accomplished it.

Then the celebrations began. Hollering and whooping, they grabbed the airplane, and lifting the tail high into the air on its mainwheels, they ran it, backward, from one end of the airstrip to the other.

And we three foreigners, who had thought mistakenly that we were in charge of this exercise, stood and watched—and smiled! This was their moment. Not ours!

I flew home a few hours later. Ray remained at Biwat to install the replacement engine that had been flown in earlier. Next day, as I was flying some hundred miles to the West, I heard on the radio, "Madang, this is Bravo Victor Kilo, taxiing Biwat for Wewak." Thirty minutes later the invincible BVK, with a new engine and a few temporary repairs, was back in our Wewak hangar. Safe and sound. It bore a decorative coating of Biwat mud—and the handprints of twenty-one men.

We made a lot of mistakes in our recovery of BVK in 1966. We nearly lost the old thing a couple of times. We ran the risk of leaving a broken, useless airframe in a faraway jungle river. But we put in a lot of effort. We dared to consider the impossible possible. It had to be done. Or at least tried. And it paid off. And this was only an airplane! A piece of machinery.

The world is littered with broken lives. On the surface they might even appear whole, but like old BVK sitting on a faraway patch of rocks in the jungle, they are dysfunctional, damaged, even lost.

And lives are of infinitely more value than airplanes. God cares about them. Every last one of them. He hears each cry for rescue, for redemption. Lost and broken people get his special attention. He will leave ninety-nine who are safe to bring back one that is lost.

That's why Jesus came.

But, unlike our stumbling attempts on the Yuat, God makes no mistakes when he is invited to lift up, repair, and rebuild. Nothing is impossible with him. He loves to redeem, to rescue, to recover.

But those who hope in the LORD will renew their strength. They will soar on wings like eagles.

ISAIAH 40:31

Do you need to be rescued ... to fly again?

Chapter
10

DESTINATION DOWNUNDER

We all have our heroes.

When I was growing up, every Australian boy knew the name Charles Kingsford-Smith. He was one of my heroes. In 1928 he made history by becoming the first man to fly across the Pacific Ocean. And he was Australian. Of course!

The story of that flight makes fascinating reading.

For more than seven thousand miles, at the breakneck speed of ninety miles per hour, he lumbered over the vast expanse of the Pacific Ocean in an old Fokker trimotor aircraft, romantically named *The Southern Cross.*

"Smithy," as he was popularly known, had an Aussie co-pilot, Charles Ulm, and an American navigator, Harry Lyon, who until that flight had only navigated ships across the ocean! Their radio operator was another American, Jim Warner.

Just picturing that ancient airplane, crawling its way through the lonely Pacific skies and over endless ocean, is mind-boggling to me. I can hardly imagine it. Twenty-seven hours from Oakland to Honolulu, and thirty-four more to Suva, in Fiji. At Suva there wasn't even an airstrip. They landed on a downtown sports ground and, after refueling, the aircraft was towed to a nearby beach for take-off. The flight from Fiji to Australia, hours of it spent in almost uncontrollable turbulence in line after line of electrical storms, was a short twenty-two hours!

Intrepid is a word that was often used in those days of the feats of amazing men, though one could say that "Smithy" and his crew were *mad*.

As for me—I dreamed of the day when I too would do it! Fly an airplane right across the Pacific Ocean!

Of course, by that time transoceanic flight was almost routine. As children, our dad would take us to Sydney's "Kingsford Smith" airport to watch the planes. Some of them would make the journey daily. But these were DC6's, Stratoclippers and Constellations—giant aircraft with inspiring names. Certainly not "rag and wire" creations like Smithy's old Fokker.

So when my chance came, there wasn't a moment's hesitation. Would I do it? Oh yes!

My "epic" flight, in 1973, was from the MAF's U.S. base at the Fullerton Municipal Airport in Orange County, Los Angeles, to Melbourne, Australia. My aircraft was to be a twin-engined Piper Aztec. Nothing fancy. And certainly not a Fokker trimotor. But enough to call for an adventuresome spirit.

This was the opportunity of a lifetime!

MAF in Australia had purchased the aircraft from a board member of MAF in the U.S. The plane was needed for mission and church work in the eastern province of Indonesia. It was to be based at Kupang, in Timor. A single-engined Cessna had been used in the initial stage of the program's development, but with so much over-water flying, a light twin would be more appropriate.

In preparation for the long flight, the four passenger seats had been removed and replaced with an enormous rubber fuel tank. This was built into a wooden frame on the cabin floor. All the connections to take the extra gas had been professionally installed and checked. We had a flight endurance of something in excess of twenty-three hours, more than enough for our longest leg.

One of MAF's senior American pilots, Hank Worthington, had agreed to make the flight with me. I don't think Hank had to be talked into it either.

We flew the airplane from Los Angeles to Oakland, California, our departure point for the first leg. This gave us the shortest track to Hawaii. On the day before the flight, not having been to San Francisco before, I took a fascinating bus tour of the city and surrounding area. As we passed by a certain part of the bay, our driver and tour guide, chattering informatively, said, "Ladies and gentlemen, this part of the bay is where the giant 'clipper' flying boats used to take off on their long journey to Honolulu. They would struggle off the water and climb ever so slowly out to the ocean. Would you believe it?" he said, "A thirteen-hour flight!" Gasps of disbelief were heard from all over the bus.

I smiled pensively and stared at the thin blue horizon. We had just completed our flight plan. The first leg? Fifteen and a half hours.

The Aztec is a very docile airplane. A good performer, it climbs well, and under normal conditions has reliable single-engine performance. In our case, an extra fuel load of more than a thousand pounds put us way beyond maximum gross weight. When I was flying jet fighters, we used to make scathing comments about aircraft with less performance than ours. "Flies like a ruptured duck," we'd snort. Hank and I were about to see just how ruptured our little duck was going to be.

"Taxi to the threshold of the short runway," the air-traffic controller said, as we requested clearance. Hank's response was crisp. "Er, we'll take the long one, thanks." We were given clearance and lined up, grossly overloaded. This was to be the longest flight I had ever made.

Take-off was surprisingly normal, and I was astonished at how quickly the aircraft became airborne. But while the plane had no problems getting off the ground, its climb performance was an entirely different matter. Foot by painstaking foot, our flying fuel tank clawed its way upward. It took a full hour to reach our chosen cruising altitude of 10,500 feet. I had read that when Kingsford-Smith departed Oakland for Hawaii, with their fuel load of four tons, they took even longer than that to reach their cruising altitude—of 1500 feet! As we entered San Francisco Bay and headed out across the mighty Pacific, I thought again of those magnificent men in their flying machines. Fifteen hundred feet was barely enough altitude to escape the ocean salt spray. Amazing courage.

"Have a safe flight," said the traffic controller as he passed us over to the area flight-service frequency.

Time crawled by—one slow hour after another. The sun was still high in the sky. Our ETA at Honolulu was 2:30 A.M. local time! We had a long way to go.

"Just follow the con-trails," the experts had said about finding one's way from San Francisco to Honolulu. "There is such a density of traffic on that route." But we saw no condensation trails. The sky was a clear, uncluttered blue. It was a magnificent day. The ocean below, however, looked more intimidating. It was littered with whitecaps. We didn't have much information about the wind at our altitude, and for all we knew it could have been blowing us miles off track. In these modern days of satellite-reading, global-positioning systems, a ferry pilot can know his exact location at any time—to within about seventy-five feet. For us it was mostly guesswork. We didn't even have good communication with the ground, and, as expected, it was not long before our one automatic direction finder (radio compass) was out of range of the coastal beacons. The needle on the instrument first began to waver and then to turn—slowly, around and around—for hour after hour.

There was a respite of sorts halfway into that fifteen-hour mix of boredom and concern. In the early seventies, a ship was stationed midway between the west coast of the U.S. and Honolulu to assist in airplane navigation. Its radio call-sign was "Ocean Station November," and great was our delight when we made contact with the radio operators who spent their time way out there in the ocean. It was reassuring to hear a human voice. It was even more reassuring to find that we were right on track and on time.

Our major concern was oil usage in the engines. Flights in an Aztec would usually average only two or three hours, thus there was no need for an oil contents gage in the cabin. But our fifteen-hour flight over the open ocean was somewhat different. Oil usage was indeed a worry.

So we just sat and waited. On and on. Strapped in. No getting up to stretch. No walking around. And all we saw was that ocean. "Flying the Pond" is the term used for such ferry flights. Some pond! And this first fifteen-hour section was only a third of the total distance across it.

What a relief when, about thirteen hours after takeoff, the radio compass needle began to respond to a beacon far ahead. It had been going round and around slowly for hours. First, almost imperceptibly, it hesitated in the "dead-ahead" position. It was beginning to recognize the Honolulu beacon. By this time it was long since dark. We could no longer see the white-caps below. The needle finally stopped. It had found the beacon. The airport, the white beach of Waikiki, coconut palms—and a bed—were out there in the darkness, waiting for us. We were nearly there.

There had been no voice contact on the radio for many hours, just the constant crackle of static. Then suddenly we heard, "Aztec Six Six Three Six Yankee, this is Honolulu Center, do you read?" What a welcome voice!

Another living soul was out there.

The flickering lights of Honolulu were a kaleidoscope of color, even at 2:00 A.M. But they didn't shine for us nearly as brightly as did the two lines of white runway lights stretching before us, guiding us down as we made our final approach.

Terra firma! We thanked God for our safe arrival.

Having been directed to the appropriate parking bay, we shut down the engines. I opened the door, took a flashlight, and jumped down onto the ground. Why did my legs feel like Jell-O and the tarmac strangely insecure? I hurried to undo the cowl flap and measure the oil contents. How much had each engine used? I really wanted to know whether our concern was justified. We didn't want to fly over even more remote stretches of ocean, constantly worried about oil consumption.

But there were almost ten quarts in each engine. We'd hardly used any oil at all. In more than fifteen hours! I sighed with relief.

An hour or so later, both of us fell into bed and were immediately lost in the blissful oblivion of deep sleep.

When we woke, we felt exhilarated. Ready for the next leg.

And so, on to Pago Pago, American Samoa, in the South Pacific.

We took off from Honolulu around noon, with a flight-planned time of sixteen and a half hours! No land mass en route. No islands—not within hundreds of miles. And this time there would be no "Ocean Station" ship positioned halfway along the route. In fact, very few airplanes of any kind crossed this particular segment of ocean.

Again, heavily laden with fuel, we fought our way to cruising altitude. The radio compass gave us a reasonable back bearing on Honolulu for about two hours. Then, we knew, for twelve hours we would have nothing until we would be able to receive transmissions from the beacon at Pago Pago. Below, huge rolling swells and monstrous waves, topped with the blowing spume from whitecaps, stretched behind and endlessly before us.

We droned on for over eight hours, tracking south from Honolulu, cocooned and uncomfortable. We had no accurate idea of our position. We were following a compass heading, but, of course, who was to know what effect the prevailing winds were having? Were we on track? Or perhaps twenty miles off? Or a hundred? There was no way of knowing and nothing we could do. Except wait for another five or six hours, when the next beacon would, hopefully, identify Pago Pago some distance out. We talked a lot but both felt the underlying tension of our situation.

Then somewhat unexpectedly a voice broke the airwaves. An airline pilot was reporting his position en route Nandi, Fiji, to Honolulu. We couldn't hear the response to his call but figured he was somewhere in our area, probably within a few hundred miles. We were not alone! We could hardly wait for him to finish his report. Then we called him up, identified ourselves, and asked him to call us back on 121.5, the short-range VHF emergency frequency. No one else could hear us using this wavelength.

"Did you say 'Aztec' Six Six Three Six Yankee?" he asked, with a southern American drawl, when we established contact on VHF.

"Affirmative."

"Do you mean a Piper Aztec? A twin-engined Piper Aztec?" His tone of voice betrayed his amazement.

"Affirmative," we again responded.

There was silence. Then, with incredulity, he asked, "Man, what are you doin' way out here? In that little-bitty airplane?"

"We're going to Australia!" Hank replied with a grin.

And so began an unforgettable radio conversation. Initially, we requested him to tilt his radar to its lowest angle, hoping he might be able to make contact with us. "We'd love to know exactly where we are." We didn't tell him we had no idea of our actual position. But he couldn't see us on his radar screen. We were disappointed.

"Tell me! What are you guys doin'?" he said. And so we told him of our flight from Oakland the previous day. Hank asked him to pass on an "operations normal" call to Honolulu Center for us. Then we talked about the great differences in our aircraft, about his four-engine jet, about his height and speed, and ours. We discussed his route, his crew, his passengers, and so on. We laughed a lot. And joked with each other.

"Hey, PanAm! How about sendin' down some of them grain-fed, three-inch Texan steaks y'all are servin' in first class!"

"Why, what are you guys eating?" he inquired.

"We're eating Fritos down here!" Hank responded. He crackled the Fritos packet close to the microphone. "Thirty-three packets and countin'!"

The 707 captain laughed. We must have chatted for thirty to forty minutes as he sped northward at about 500 knots, and we, far below, lumbered on southward at about 120. Finally he said goodbye. That contact with another human voice had been wonderfully therapeutic in our lonely, exposed flight.

About five minutes later, however, we heard that friendly voice again.

"Hey, Aztec! You still there?" Hank smiled at me.

"I've been talkin' to my girls about you." (We assumed he meant the stewardesses on his crew.) "We're a bit concerned. We reckon if we was you, and you was us, we'd like you to keep on talkin' for a while. So let's keep this thing goin'!"

And he went on to tell us about a fishing lodge he had on Victoria Island, off Vancouver, and the Cessna 180 seaplane he "played with" when he was there. He told us about the families of all his crew, where they came from, what they did for relaxation. Trivia, but much appreciated entertainment.

We in turn told him about MAF and its unique use of airplanes in mission.

Our conversation continued until we began to lose contact with each other because of the widening distance between us. Eventually, the transmissions began to break up, and we signed off.

Once again, the hours went slowly by.

In loneliness, in isolation, the power of a human voice is profound. Hank and I wondered, as we flew along, how many people, probably millions right at that moment, longed to hear a human voice. Not people exposed to the kind of extreme isolation we were experiencing, but people sitting in homes, in apartments, perhaps in some of the busiest places on earth. We had friends, loved ones, who were waiting and praying for us. But who cared for all these others? In that time of absolute isolation, we realized how powerfully effective a human voice can be.

Someone once wrote, "What is life to one for whom no one waits?" What, indeed.

Night came on. A pitch-black, cloudless Pacific night. The stars were crystal clear and quite brilliant. We watched a satellite slowly make its way across the heavens and wondered whether it might be a space capsule. Perhaps someone was up there, like us sitting in cramped isolation, far from home.

It was easy and natural to think about God. The astounding thought, as we droned our way slowly across that mighty ocean under a canopy of those millions of bright, shining stars, was that God knew precisely where we were. He didn't need a puny manmade global positioning system. He knew—exactly— and he did care.

We felt safe.

Eventually, as it had the previous night, the searching needle of the radio compass once more began to indicate that there was a beacon out there ahead of us, hundreds of miles away. Initially again, it hesitated from its monotonous circling, at the "right on the nose" position, and finally caught the pulse of a signal. After a few more rotations it settled happily to a stop, pointing to our destination out there in the darkness. Pago Pago! Only a little place. But oh, how welcome!

And so we landed there at about 3:00 A.M. on a balmy tropical night.

Having eventually found a hotel, we once again flopped onto our beds and were soon peacefully asleep. We didn't realize until about 10:00 A.M. that we had been taken to a glitzy tourist resort and the entire wall of our room was glass—right at sand-level! Outside was a glorious, wide, sun-drenched tropical beach. The blue sea glistened in the morning sun, fifty yards away. The curtains were totally open, and tanned-skinned, beautiful people traipsed by, curiously looking in at two semi-clad men draped over the beds, sound asleep in the middle of the morning. How fortunate that we had not entirely disrobed in our exhaustion.

The flight to Auckland, New Zealand, later that day was relatively short. Only ten hours. As we flew over Vavah'u, a northern island of the Kingdom of Tonga, we looked down on dozens of yachts moored in the magnificent bay there. Vavah'u is a haven for oceanic "yacht-ies." We wondered what they thought of us as we passed overhead.

Rain was bucketing down when we landed at Auckland International Airport to be met by friends from MAF New Zealand. A layover of twenty-four hours and the company of these good people were a welcome interlude. Rain was still falling when we departed the following day for Melbourne. Was this an omen?

The meteorological office in Auckland could not tell us with any accuracy the wind speed at ten thousand feet, our proposed altitude for the last part of our journey. They did know that there were reports of severe weather over the Tasman Sea. "It's a slow-moving system and seems to be stuck out there," they told us. "If you were flying at thirty-five thousand feet, we would have more accurate weather for you, but airline pilots are reporting significant buildups mid-Tasman. Reports of occasional lightning."

Significant buildups? Occasional lightning?

By the time we had trundled five hours out across the ocean, Hank and I were in one accord. The New Zealand meteorological officers had been just a tad conservative. By then, "significant" and "occasional" had become "horrendous" and "unrelenting." There were brilliant flashes all around us. Without radar, the best we could do was simply head for the area of the sky that seemed to be least affected by towering, violent electrical storms. But there was no avoiding them.

It made no sense to turn around and fly back to Auckland. Huge thunderheads, filled with bursts of intense white light, completely encircled us. We pressed on.

The entire region of the mid-Tasman that night was a mass of turbulent weather. Each time we entered cloud, massive bursts of hissing, roaring electricity flashed around, illuminating the entire sky. Sizzling bolts of power exploded into the boiling sea below. The Aztec itself appeared aglow, like a neon tube. I'd seen this phenomenon before. St. Elmo's fire. Static electricity painted circles of fire around the tips of the propellers, while snaking worms of electricity raced over the windscreen and around the cabin glass.

Worst of all was the turbulence. Although we had the automatic pilot engaged, it was all we could do to simply hold the aircraft straight and level. We were thrown from side to side, at one moment being pressed down into our seats, the next, weightless! The airplane felt like a leaf being blown around in a storm. The experience was at once extremely dangerous and incredibly exhilarating. In the excitement of the thunder, the sizzling streaks of lightning, and the impossibly violent turbulence, we lost all thought of the risk. It was the ride of a lifetime!

We couldn't read the compass, but it didn't matter. Whether we were forced to divert to the right or left of track was somewhat immaterial. After all, we were not likely to miss Australia! So for more than two hours we just hung on and fought to keep the plane in the air.

At one point, I recall thinking, "Mr. Piper, you made a sturdy aircraft when you made this Aztec." It just kept plowing on through the storms, hail, and horrendous buffeting. Not once did we detect even the slightest sound of discord in the note of those two engines. They just sang on, in harmony, almost as if they were as determined to complete the journey as the two men struggling at the controls.

Then, suddenly, after about two or three hours, we burst out of the western side of that band of awe-inspiring storms into calm, smooth air.

Soon the coastline of eastern Victoria came into view. Long stretches of yellow sand and the endless lines of crashing white breakers marked the "ninety-mile" beach. Inland, Victoria's eastern lakes and heavily timbered mountains painted a tranquil and beautiful scene.

Home! Australia!

The landing at Essendon Airport was uneventful, almost an anticlimax. Jo was there with a few MAF friends to meet us. We soon had the aircraft cleared by the customs officials, and I was on the way home—for a good long rest. My five boys were fascinated with the tale I had to tell.

I'd done it! At last. But never again!

I never looked for the opportunity to do it again.

"Smithy," in the *Southern Cross*, spent eighty-three hours in the air on his remarkable journey. It took us just fifty-five!

With hardly an hour or two to catch his breath, my friend Hank went out to the International Airport at Melbourne and caught a plane back to the U.S.! Hank was tougher than I.

I have often reflected on that crossing. It was a wonderful, unforgettable experience. I had always dreamed of making such a flight. We flew a considerable distance around the world in a tiny little airplane. Just a brave little dot, winging its way over the sea.

And as I've looked back upon it, I have thought about how small and insignificant we were, squeezed into a tiny cabin, unable to get out of our seats or even to get up to stretch. So vulnerable. Had there been a mechanical failure out there somewhere, someone might have found us. But it would have been unlikely.

Did anyone know precisely where we were?

God knew.

He tells us that he knows even when a sparrow falls to the ground.

People are more valuable than sparrows. And God knows each and every one. Wherever we are, and in whatever predicament. When we long to hear another human voice, when loneliness eats its way to the depth of our being and we are buffeted and losing control, surely one of life's greatest treasures is to hear an inner voice guiding us home, reminding us.

"I will never leave you nor forsake you."

JOSHUA 1:5

And the Spirit of God was hovering over the waters.

GENESIS 1:2

Chapter

11

THANKS BUT NO THANKS

To feel appreciated is a basic human need.

And a simple "Thank you," easy to say, means so much. To give thanks is more than good manners. It is a gift.

We never lacked for "thank yous" in mission aviation. Our service was always deeply appreciated by church and mission, and by the community at large. So often we were their lifeline to the outside world, mountain and jungle barriers broken down by our little Cessnas. And gratitude was expressed in wonderful and creative ways. Perhaps it was homemade lemonade and cake served on the tailplane. Just to say thank you.

Sometimes one dear lady, with great care, would drape a white lace tablecloth over the metal surface and artistically arrange morning or afternoon tea, in true British tradition. Bone china cups, delicately made little sandwiches—even a silver teapot! All surrounded by hundreds of near-naked, stone-age warriors!

Almost every day we would bring something home from someone. A paw-paw, a bunch of bananas, fresh vegetables, sometimes even strawberries or roses, unknown on the coast but grown successfully at high altitudes. "Take these home to Jo," would be the request. "Tell her, 'thank you!'"

———

There were almost always thanks in the pain-filled eyes of patients being lifted into the plane to fly to a distant hospital base. Without that evacuation flight there would be nothing ahead but more pain, and probably death. It might only be those eyes that expressed appreciation with a glance or a look. At other times, "thank you" was expressed almost inaudibly through lips clenched in deep agony and spoken in a language we could not understand.

Such gratitude made our job all the more fulfilling.

———

Thanks!

Of all the "thank yous" I have ever received for a flight, one stands out above all others. It wasn't tea on the tailplane. It wasn't fruit or flowers.

For Laurie Darrington and me this flight was unique. In fact, we risked the suspension of our flying licenses by doing it.

We flew a small boy back to his island home, more than a hundred and twenty miles off the north coast of New Guinea. We took him home. To die.

This desperately ill child, about twelve years of age, had been brought into the Wewak District Hospital by a Russian oceanographic survey ship. The Russians had found him on an island called Ninigo, and they had brought him to Wewak where they knew there was a good hospital. But nothing could be done for him. He had advanced leukemia. There was no treatment.

"Couldn't you possible fly him home?" Risto Gobius, the district medical office and hospital superintendent, kept asking. "There won't be a boat going out there for months. It would have been better if he had not been brought here. He cries all day and half the night. There's no one here who can speak his language. We can't explain to him that he's going to die. It's so sad. He needs to be with people he knows and loves. You've got a seaplane. Can't you help?"

But we couldn't get approval to do a flight like that. No one had ever flown an airplane to Ninigo Island. There was little contact with Ninigo other than through a small trading boat that collected the annual copra harvest.

My good friend Risto was very persuasive. "Max, please. Just come out to the hospital and see this kid," he pleaded.

"It can't be done, Risto," I said. But he was insistent.

I finally went. And when I saw the little boy, I knew immediately that it should be done. It had to be done. Risto, Laurie, and I would take him.

The day was particularly beautiful. The sea was a deep blue, and wispy clouds flecked the tranquil sky. Beside us on the floor lay our frail little patient. His wasted body was covered in bruise-like lesions, and there were traces of blood around his mouth. Our hearts ached for him.

A vast expanse of ocean had to be crossed. This certainly was not a normal operation. We were looking for an island that none of us had ever seen and where no airplane had ever been before.

What an exquisite little place Ninigo turned out to be. A flat, palm-covered green island, it was outlined on one side with clean white sand, on the other with a white line where the gentle breaking surf washed over a coral reef. The water was crystal clear. A resort developer would have been ecstatic! Imagine the potential of this glorious, unspoiled paradise.

There was no smooth water lagoon that we could see. As we circled, we must have attracted the astonished attention of every villager on Ninigo. An airplane? Over our island? It was unheard of. They were beside themselves with excitement—waving, shouting, jumping. We flew around, trying to find a safe length of quiet water shoreward of the encircling reef. But there was none. Eventually, having noticed the sea was quite calm, I decided to land outside the reef and taxi the aircraft over it, to the beach. We had noticed that the village was near the shoreline.

A group of huge men appeared, running toward the beach from among the nearby coconut trees. They splashed their way through the water to meet us. I cut the engine quickly and steered the aircraft to the shallows. As the first of the men reached us they began to clamber up onto the float. We had to gesture and yell to them to keep clear. A dozen heavy men on one float of a seaplane is a recipe for disaster.

Their obvious leader shouted orders and instructions to the others. We motioned for him, on his own, to climb up onto the pontoon. Then we opened the plane's door.

When he saw the child on the floor, he gasped and uttered a low moan. Instantly, his joy turned to sadness. He turned back and spoke to his men, who were excitedly waiting their turn to see into this strange machine. They were immediately silent. Turning back to the dying boy, he gently and compassionately stroked his face and hair, murmuring soft, comforting words.

For the first time in weeks, the little fellow smiled. He was home.

Two of the men ran off and returned, minutes later, with a large woven mat. They draped it over the aircraft float, and we gently lowered the boy onto it. What followed was a strange and moving ritual.

In absolute silence, like pallbearers, they carried him high above the crystal clear, warm blue water, to the shore. Then, with soft and harmonious wailing, they moved in solemn procession, off through the trees. We could still hear them long after they were out of sight. These were a deeply grieving people.

We waded around in the shallow waters for a few minutes, not sure what to do next. It didn't seem right for us to intrude. What we had set out to do, out of mercy for a dying boy, had been done. We felt satisfied. But it was strangely anticlimactic for the three of us, standing there alone by the shore.

"Well, we may as well go home," one of us said rather flatly.

But as we were turning the aircraft around and preparing to climb back into it, the village chief appeared again through the trees. With him were a few others. They walked at a solemn pace along the beach, as if on a ceremonial parade. They weren't running, as they had been when we arrived. There were no yells of excitement as they waded to where we were standing by our gently bobbing seaplane.

One by one, they encircled us until we were completely surrounded. Each one of them gently touched us, on our arms and shoulders. It was as if, through physical contact, they felt we could be joined in spirit.

Then the chief, a huge brown man, looked directly at us and with great emotion in his deep resonant voice. *"Mipela tok tenkyu."* ("We say thank you.")

That was all. But it was enough. They waited in silence for a few extra moments. Then these dignified island men turned away again and made their way back to the village, no doubt to join in the grieving and sorrow. I felt like crying. What a "thank you" that was. What a gift.

I doubt that I will ever go back to Ninigo or see its pristine beauty again. But I am left with an image of an exquisite little tropical island and, somewhere, a small grave in the sand.

But No Thanks!

My little Cessna was exposed, vulnerable, and totally out of place. Another towering gray-green wave, capped with white, bore down upon it. As the airplane's nose rose to climb the face of this massive volume of water, the propeller bit into the swirling white cap with a crunching sound and drove high-speed missiles of salt water all over the windscreen and wings.

In the troughs between the unending succession of swells, there appeared to be nothing but ocean surrounding me. But from the crest of each wave, I could make out the lines of coconut palms on the distant shore.

What in the world was I doing here? In this little seaplane? On an angry ocean?

———

Close to midnight on the previous evening, a group of men had come to our house saying that a small boat was missing along the coast to the west of Wewak. Two men from their fishing club had not returned, they told us. There was a chalkboard by the boat ramp, and every group going beyond the confines of the Wewak bay was required to record where they were intending to fish and the time they planned to return. People seldom stayed out after their nominated return time.

These two men had gone out early in the day, intending to fish along the coast to the west, within twenty miles of the town. They had written on the board that they expected to be back at 6:00 P.M. But by 9:00 P.M., when they hadn't arrived, it was obvious that something was wrong.

"We'll wait all night for them" the men said to us. "But if they haven't turned up by daylight, could you please search the area for us and try to find out where they are? Perhaps you could get the plane ready so that you could be in the air right at first light? We feel it's very serious. These guys never stay out late," they said.

The missing boat didn't return during the night.

Next morning, just before dawn, several of us drove to the Wewak market, at the leeward beach of the town, where we kept our floatplane. Normally at this time of day there was a bustle of activity. Local village women would be gathering with their bags of smoked fish and flying fox, bananas and mangoes, pineapples and paw paws, beetle nut, coconuts, and limes, laying them out on woven mats for the day's trading. But it was Sunday and the market was deserted. I parked the MAF van.

The yellow and black seaplane presented an incongruous sight, tied to a trailer on the sand beside the empty market stalls. It had become something of an attraction, but it was safe and secure, nonetheless. In those days, at least.

As the sun began to lighten the eastern sky, we pushed the trailer into the water and floated the seaplane free. I climbed aboard, completed my pre-takeoff checks, started the engine, and taxied very carefully through the calm, shallow water barely covering the nearby coral reef, and into the deeper part of the bay. I had removed all the seats from the aircraft to keep it as light as possible, in case I had to land in the open sea.

As I took off I noticed that, unlike the smoother water in the lee of the Wewak headland, the outer ocean was running a heavy swell. A thorough scattering of whitecaps suggested it was not a day to be out in a fourteen-foot aluminum dinghy. Nor was it a day to land a small floatplane, designed for calm waters, in the open sea. Many times we had operated that Cessna in conditions for which I'm sure it was never designed. I had put it down in narrow, swiftly running rivers and even on the ocean. But never in a sea like this.

I flew the prescribed area at two thousand feet about five miles from the coast. There was no sign of a small boat anywhere. With the coast still in sight, I decided to fly on a little farther before heading back and beginning a more "patterned" search.

At the end of that extra leg I saw the boat. It was miles beyond where I had been told it should be, and in spite of the patches of white on the ocean, it was surprisingly visible in the morning sun. I descended and flew toward it.

The boat was upright but full of water, wallowing in the heavy sea. Only the back was not submerged. Sitting there, on the stern plank, was a man. His head was drooping on his chest and with every roll of the boat it flopped and he would tip, almost falling back into the water. He neither looked up nor waved, even though I flew close by, barely ten feet above the waves. There was no outboard motor. It appeared that at some stage during the night the boat had capsized and the motor with everything else on board had gone to the bottom of the ocean.

It was on my second pass that I noticed the body of the other man, rolling and bobbing in the front of the water-filled boat. My heart sank.

The survivor, wearing no life jacket, was obviously close to the end of his endurance. Clearly, there was little chance for him. Unless something drastic was done. A rescue boat would take hours to get to this position from Wewak.

I was utterly perplexed. To even attempt a landing in these mountainous seas would be madness. But could it be done? I looked hard at the lines of swells and wondered, if indeed I did manage to pull off a landing, how I would ever get airborne again. And how could I get that fellow on board anyway. I was on my own! I would have to climb down out of the cockpit to help him. Who would control the aircraft? I prayed desperately.

This man's life was in my hands.

I tried to judge the height of the waves. I looked at the waterlogged boat to see how it rose and fell. I even counted the frequency of the breaking swells. Whitecaps looked pretty from higher up. Now they were angry and ominous.

Nonetheless, I was fairly sure I could get down. And I felt I had a better than even chance of at least getting the man out of the boat and on board. But I was far from sure that I could take off again. *Perhaps*, I thought, *I can land, pick him up, and then just taxi to the lee of the small island I had noticed a few miles away.* But even taxiing in such conditions would be extremely demanding, if not impossible. The wind was blowing right across the swells. Any takeoff would have to be made crosswind along the swells. In a sea as heavy as this, it would be an extremely risky procedure.

I was also worried about the aircraft's propeller. I had seen before the effect upon a propeller when impacted by saltwater at high speed. The leading edge of the blade rapidly splits, almost folding it open.

But how could I just fly back to Wewak, leaving this man alone in a disabled boat, to die? With a pounding heart, I determined to try to rescue him.

I reduced power, configured the aircraft for landing, and set up my approach. I had to land crosswind, along the heaving swell lines. At the first smack of dark-green ocean water, I jerked the throttle closed and pulled back hard on the control column. The plane stopped quickly.

Almost immediately, the aircraft tilted 45 degrees as it rode sideways up one swell, and perched for a split second high on the water. I could see the coast. But then, with the same degree of "bank," this time to the port, I slid down the other face of the wave.

It was very difficult to taxi. In spite of pressure to the rudders, the waves and wind tugged at the aircraft, seeking to "weathercock" it into the wind. I was also aware that colliding with the edges of the metal boat would quickly puncture the floats. Finally, I managed to position myself as close as I dared alongside the waterlogged dinghy. It was too heavy to ride over the top of the swells, and every broken whitecap threatened to wash the fisherman from his perch in the stern.

Suddenly, with a start, he became conscious of my presence. An airplane? Out here on the water? It must have been beyond his belief. He immediately tried to stand up and reach toward me.

"Sit down!" I yelled through the open window, against the noise of the engine. "Don't try to get up. I'll come alongside. Don't do anything until you hear my engine stop. Then jump for the plane. I'll get you."

He understood. His ashen face bore a mixed expression of fear, hope, and desperation.

As I approached the boat on the third try, I cut the engine, opened the door, and jumped out onto the float. It was wet and slick. I felt exposed and vulnerable as the wind buffeted me and the spray whipped at my face. *What will happen if I fall into the water?* I thought. Now uncontrolled, the airplane immediately began to turn into the wind, pointing its nose at the oncoming swells. "Now, jump!" I screamed. He did so, and I grabbed his jacket at the neck and pulled him across the float. He lay there for a moment while I clung to the strut. Then, with great difficulty, I manhandled his sodden body on board and scrambled in after him.

Safe! Well, at least, away from the water.

Climbing quickly into my seat I turned the ignition key. "Please, God, let it start," I prayed. The engine roared into life again. The whirling propeller spat water across the windshield. *Whatever are those propeller blades like?* I worried, as I turned to taxi once more along the swells. I hadn't even thought to check. I prayed that they were not too damaged. There was nothing I could do about it anyway.

My passenger by this time was sitting at the back of the cabin on the floor with his head up against of the rear bulkhead.

I taxied by the boat once more. I felt awful leaving that body, rolling around in the water, caught in the boat's super-structure. But any more effort to recover it would have been foolish in the extreme. Feeling heavyhearted, I turned the airplane away.

There were still grave doubts that we could get airborne again. An island five miles to the east was probably within reach, but I could see now that taxiing there was impossible. Fortunately I had used a good quantity of fuel and the aircraft, lighter now, was sitting higher in the water. I advised Wewak that I was getting airborne again, and once more lined the plane up along the swells.

At first, even with full power, it didn't seem as if we were going to move. With each massive wave, one wing would drop as we climbed the lee side, and then in a lazy roll, the other would fall away as we slipped down the face.

Sheets of water poured over the engine and wings as the airplane began to move. The airspeed indicator wasn't registering anything at all. The pitot head—the external airspeed sensor—was full of seawater.

With the engine screaming, and undoubtedly with spray flying in a gigantic plume behind us, the seaplane began to pick up speed. Between wave tops we would accelerate further, only to have the momentum decrease as we ploughed through a crest. I could only hope and pray that eventually, we might become airborne.

Suddenly, we were suspended, barely, in the air as we leapt from the top of a huge swell. Perhaps it was not so much that the plane got airborne but rather that the water underneath just dropped away! With my right hand I grabbed a couple of "notches" of flap. I thought we were going to hit again at the bottom of the next trough. But we didn't, and the airplane clawed its way over the oncoming wall of water.

The airspeed indicator still read zero. The system was indeed blocked with sea water. But we really were flying! I reported my departure to Wewak and gave them an estimate for arrival at the town beach.

"Request report on the state of the survivors," was their quick response.

"Wewak, there is only one survivor," I replied. They did not ask for a name or for more information.

Back on the smooth water of the bay, I taxied toward the small crowd waiting on the beach behind the marketplace. I was so grateful to God and thankful to be safely back.

Two women stood thigh-deep in the water. Both were waiting for their husbands. It was heart-wrenching. The memory of a partly submerged, bluish body out there in the ocean haunted me. Who was he? What was he like? Which of these two women was his wife?

Jo drove me home from the beach that Sunday. I was exhausted. It was so good to be back. The plane needed a thorough wash-down and a new propeller. Otherwise it was fine. The Cessna. What a marvelous airplane.

All that afternoon I wondered what was happening in the town. How were they going to recover the body? How was the man I had rescued? It would be good to talk with him. On the flight back to Wewak he had told me that they had caught a lot of fish during the afternoon; there were large bags of them in the center of the boat. But broadside to a huge freak wave, the bags of fish had suddenly slipped right across the floor and the craft had capsized. The motor was torn from its mounting and immediately sank. The restraining chain had snapped.

Unfortunately, the bucket in which they had placed all the required emergency gear was not secured, and also disappeared into the rising sea. Then darkness fell.

His friend had died during the night and the survivor, so traumatized by the shocking experience, had become quite hallucinatory. He told me that hundreds of sea snakes had come into the boat as it filled with water and had killed his friend. I did hear later, however, that it was revealed that his mate had died from a heart attack.

During the next few days I fully expected someone to come, at least to talk to me about the events of that morning. Perhaps, even, to say thank you.

But no one ever came.

Maybe the survivor had left town quickly. No doubt the awful shock and trauma of the experience would have had a devastating effect on him. I never heard from him again. Not a word.

And as the years have gone by, the memory of it has always seemed, somehow, unfinished.

———

These are stories about one life that was saved and two that were lost. But they are really stories about giving thanks. They illustrate a basic human need. To be affirmed. To be appreciated. To be thanked. Even Jesus felt hurt when only one leper came back to thank him for the healing he had received. "Where are the other nine?" Jesus asked.

The psalmist knew a lot about saying thank you. Over and over he calls us to give thanks to God for all that he has done. "Enter his gates with thanksgiving and his courts with praise; give thanks to him and praise his name" (Psalm 100:4).

It is the same in the New Testament. "Be joyful always; pray continually; give thanks in all circumstances, for this is God's will for you in Christ Jesus" (1 Thessalonians 5:16–18).

The people at Ninigo, even in their grief, came back to say, "*Tenkyu*." And we felt wonderfully rewarded.

Have you thanked anyone lately?

Have you thanked God lately?

Chapter

12

CROSSROADS AND INTERSECTIONS

At some of life's "crossroads" there is little or no choice.

For those I saw in the feeding camps of Ethiopia in the middle eighties, there was no choice. For them, it was come and be fed. Or die.

I met a man there. He had faced a choice. To stay home and certainly die or walk for more than a hundred miles across the hot, drought-ravaged wasteland with his wife and six children to find food and medical attention. So he chose. Already weakened by starvation and knowing that there was little chance of them all surviving, they began to walk. Mile after mile across the parched and barren landscape, he led his family. Along the way, one by one, they succumbed. First his wife, then a child. Then another. And another. Four crude graves marked his family's trek to find help. Toward the end, this courageous father would carry one child for a quarter of a mile, place it under any shade he could find, then go back for another. And thus, in this relay of agony and desperation, he reached the camp.

A desperate choice.

———

In Port au Prince, Haiti, I once saw a mother squatting in the middle of the road, reaching down with a battered saucepan through a sewer access. Fetid, stagnant water was all she could find to pour over the feverish body of her small baby. A world away, in Dhaka, Bangladesh, I have seen other mothers and children at night, begging and crying out for food in the dark, crowded streets. They didn't choose to be born into that environment. They didn't choose these conditions from which they had no escape. For some, life offers few choices.

———

We make our decisions day after day, as the years go by. Barely perceptible, the direction of our life is slowly developed, sculptured by the choices we make. They create our memories, fill our scrapbooks, and mold our future. One decision becomes the platform upon which the next and the next is made. And so our life's direction is formed.

Most of us can look back to choices made in the immaturity of youth that have significant ramifications for us as adults. I've already mentioned my choice not to take seriously the learning of Latin in school. It was a little thing, not of earth-shattering importance. But it robbed me of the opportunity to learn something valuable. And shortly after that I made another choice—to leave school altogether. That had far greater implications for my life.

———

Often, when choices are made by the powerful, who are motivated by evil and ambition, the results are sweeping and devastating. Millions—entire nations and cultures—suffer. All over the world we see lives everywhere that have been devastated by decisions of others. Unwanted and abused children. Persecuted and starving people. Refugees. Child soldiers. Victims of hatred and greed—the list is endless. A simple but poignant example of this stands out for me.

Enver Hoxja, the long-ruling communist dictator of Albania had declared his country an atheistic state. God did not exist, he said, and beginning at the end of World War II, with terrifying aggression, Hoxja had set out to expunge the mere notion of God from the soul of the Albanian people. For forty-seven years he wreaked havoc on those who had no option but to follow. Merely owning a Bible or discussing religion could lead to years of imprisonment. People were encouraged to inform on one another. Family member on family member, neighbor on neighbor. Fear gripped the nation. Perhaps most sinister of all, people were taught—driven—to think the worst of others. There was no trust. Only suspicion. Radical communism, fueled by fear and terror, was the mark of Albanian life. Children born in those years knew no other way. Thus a generation emerged with no understanding of the fundamental human right to exercise choice.

In 1990, when the doors of this ancient biblical nation of Illyricum began to open, Mission Aviation Fellowship (MAF) went there to be involved in relief, not aviation. Mainly, we facilitated the supply and distribution of hospital equipment and medicines. Drug stores in Albania were all but empty. One hospital we visited had no more drugs on its pharmacy shelves than one would find in the majority of bathroom closets of any home in the West.

We quickly realized the material, moral, spiritual bankruptcy of the country.

As president of MAF, I was invited to sit in on a meeting with the minister for health. He and some of his staff were to meet with the North American organization with which we were associated, involved in bringing medical supplies into Albania.

The minister had a strong complaint. The actual value of pharmaceuticals that had been shipped to Albania from the West was far less than had been publicized in the United States.

"You were quoted in the international press as having brought two million dollars worth of medicines to Albania," he said. "This is simply not true. I could purchase everything on the inventory for about half that amount on the open market. I have been accused of graft and corruption because people think I have somehow made off with the difference!"

His complaint was reasonable. The foreign group was valuing the shipment at Western retail prices, in spite of the fact that a good deal of it had been donated at no cost at all. Many relief organizations use this procedure. The higher figure encourages further giving. It is an expedient practice and not dishonest. It makes good press. The end result is that more relief supplies can be provided.

Communication quickly degenerated. Each man defended his own position, in an argument that grew in intensity and heat. The longer the conversation continued, the more bitter and angry it became, the Albanians seeming so aggressive, totally unbending and unreasonable.

It was a tragic moment. Those who stood in such desperate need, and those who were both willing and able to provide, were drawing farther and farther apart from each other.

As the meeting was closing, I asked the minister if I could make an observation. I explained that the division I had seen between them was based on a relatively unimportant issue, but it was driving a wedge between the two parties that could deprive the Albanian people of great help. And yet it was their leaders who were the more closed-minded and combative.

Sometimes, I explained, differences can be swept aside just by us being open-minded to another person's perspective. Presuming the best in people rather than the worst, avoiding suspicion, and trying to understand, is often the pathway to greater opportunity. I talked to him of the principle of "standing in another man's shoes, and that to do so was his choice."

It puzzled me that he did not seem to understand how much he had to lose by arguing over a somewhat trivial matter. His people were in desperate need, yet it seemed he was shutting off a source of immense assistance, due simply to an unwillingness to bend, compromise, or even choose to listen. I hoped he had not taken offense. He was, after all, a leader in the government of Albania.

A few nights later, we hosted Albanian dignitaries at the Hotel Tirana. That night, the minister sought me out. "Mr. Meyers, I want to tell you something that I learned this week, through you," he said.

"In our society," he said, "we have not been taught to think the best of anyone. We have not been taught to listen. We do not negotiate. We do not trust. We certainly do not even try to understand an opposing viewpoint. For my people, this is a sign of weakness that will result in defeat. Perhaps, in generations gone by, we may have acted differently. But not now. Not for many decades."

He paused.

"Your comments really got to me. I see that there is an enormous weakness in Albanian culture. You made me examine attitudes that I've always accepted as normal. What you said was new, challenging, and liberating."

His final comment was profound.

"I realize now, for the first time, that I can *choose* how I treat other people. This will change my life."

I could hardly believe what he was saying.

———

There was so much social and material decay in Albania. So much sadness. Such a spiritual vacuum. A despotic leader had chosen to eradicate every influence of the Creator-God. He had robbed the people of a basic human right—to make choices for themselves. The product was a soulless nation of atheism and emptiness. And the entire culture—millions of people—suffered the awful consequences.

But now, this Albanian minister of health was rediscovering a precious truth.

It is God who gives us freedom to choose. We are created to choose.

———

Joshua, one of history's greatest leaders, at the end of his life gathered the people together and, beginning with the story of Abraham, he recounted to them all that God had done for them down through the ages. "If serving the LORD seems undesirable to you," he said, "then choose for yourselves this day whom you will serve. . . . But as for me and my household, we will serve the LORD."

And the people responded, "We too will serve the LORD, because he is our God" (Joshua 24:15–18).

We are not like automatons once we yield to God. He doesn't make our decisions for us. Life is not like some great slot-car race where the entire course is prescribed for us and we have no options available. Rather, he lays before us, every day, choices that provide the opportunities for us to develop into the people he wants us to be. Making choices, choosing, is something that has to be learned.

Henri Nouwen said a lot about choice:

> I am becoming aware that there are few moments without the opportunity to choose. . . . One aspect of

choosing life is choosing joy. Joy is life-giving, but sadness brings death. . . .

I am convinced that we can choose joy. Every moment we can decide to respond to an event or a person with joy instead of sadness . . . to choose joy does not mean to choose happy feelings or an artificial atmosphere of hilarity. But it does mean the determination to let whatever takes place bring us one step closer to the God of life.

I am called to be joyful. It gives much consolation to know that I can choose joy."

Eternity is also a matter of choice. And it is ours to make.

Choose life, so that you and your children may live and that you may love the LORD your God, listen to his voice, and hold fast to him. For the LORD is your life.
DEUTERONOMY 30:19–20

We make our choices—and our choices make us!

Make good choices. Choose life. Choose joy. Choose Christ. Choose God.

Chapter
13

TOP DOG

A reception and dinner in our honor at a foreign embassy, in a Muslim country, was not a common occurrence for me.

The venue was impressive, the large reception area beautifully decorated. The people, too, were impressive. Cabinet members and leading figures from the national parliament were there with their wives. Ambassadors and dignitaries from other countries made it a truly multicultural gathering. The exquisite national dress of the women added brilliant color to the evening. It was a glittering occasion.

A year or so earlier, in a discussion there with government leaders about aviation needs in the country, I had suggested that MAF could significantly contribute to the further development of the country's transportation infrastructure. And so we were there to inaugurate the program that had eventuated from those discussions. We were to provide "grassroots" aviation services, particularly to assist in medical evacuation, the transportation of development staff working in such fields as agriculture and education, and, especially, in disaster relief.

It provided an opportunity to live and work in a predominantly Islamic society. At the meeting during the previous year, I had explained MAF's uniqueness in the aviation business. A not-for-profit organization, professional and very experienced in general aviation, we were, at the same time, followers of Jesus. I told them that we would not preach on street corners or build Christian churches in the towns, but it would be an honor for us to make a contribution to the development and well-being of the people. We would not come, however, if we were expected to suppress or deny our allegiance to Jesus. I said, "Let us model for you the love of Jesus rather than preach it in the streets."

Their response had surprised me. To them it was most unusual for someone to bring aviation expertise as a service to the people—in the name of God—and not as a profit-making venture. While we were not required to hide our Christian motivation, we had to be wise in expressing it. This was indeed a new kind of challenge for MAF.

At the nationally televised inauguration ceremony earlier that day, the president of the nation had warmly welcomed us as friends. And the embassy reception was a celebration of the launching. Our newly appointed manager and his wife were with us for the occasion.

I stood talking to a group of men. An ambassador from the Middle East was interested in what we were doing. "I wish you would come with me to my country and present a similar proposal," he said. "Our international airline is very successful. It has services all over the world, but it really only caters to the rich, to international business, to the oil industry, government, and a few tourists. We don't know how to touch the common people of our country through aviation the way you have done in so many places." I could hardly believe what he was asking. His nation was at the very heart of Islam.

Almost everyone was positive. Except just one. There had been no affirmation from him. He was aggressive. A senior government official of the host nation, he spent a considerable time telling me about his excellent academic qualifications—a Ph.D. from Britain as well as other degrees. He told me about his work in seeking foreign aid. "That squadron of Russian MIGs you saw at the airport," he said with pride, "I organized for us to get them."

As he continued, his confrontational manner drove the others in our little group subtly away. They left him to me. Clearly, they knew him. Having spent some time "presenting" himself, he startled me with a direct question. It was an obvious set-up.

"What do you think about the current president of the United States?"

I was an Australian, working at that time out of Australia. I had no intention of being dragged into a conversation like this.

"Well, Doctor," I said, trying to evade the question, "what do *you* think about the U.S. president?" Fortunately he took my lead. He began a long, very negative diatribe about the American leader of the day and upon the United States as a whole. "He's power mad. America is always motivated by power, by a passion to control. It manipulates nations like ours by offering what is presented as aid and compassion when the underlying strategy is to extend the influence of its power. Always power, always control. Accepting their so-called 'aid' is very costly for us in terms of our own national dignity."

Obviously he didn't think much of the United States of America.

I was very uncomfortable, but he had me cornered.

"Doctor," I responded, "you've said some tough things about America. But earlier you told me that you negotiated the deployment of the squadron of Russian MIG fighters I saw at the airport. So clearly you've been to Moscow as well. What comments do you have about Russian leadership?"

"Just as bad. Just as corrupt," he replied. I was surprised. "Just another kind of power play and manipulation. It costs us heavily in terms of independence and feelings of self-worth." I listened as he then shared his opinions of the current Russian leaders.

"Well," I said, "now, let me ask you something. You see weaknesses in other models. What about your own leadership? Having seen the bad in others, what better things are done by your own leaders? How do they lead this nation and its people?"

He responded, almost with disdain for my question. "You are an international person. I'm sure you make your own comparisons as you come here. You can see our incredible problems. We can't lead our country as we would like to. We're grossly overpopulated. We can't even provide enough food for the people. Children go hungry. We have no industry to speak of. Even paying the interest on our national debt is killing us. We almost entirely depend on the giving, the largesse, of the powerful nations. We don't get on with our neighbors. We are in a bind between our awesome need and our fear of being manipulated and controlled. We struggle constantly, for survival."

Thank God, I thought. We were slowly but surely getting away from the U.S. president!

"You know, Doctor," I commented, "there's a far broader subject to discuss than the leadership of the U.S. or of Russia. And it seems to me we are in agreement. There is a global crisis of leadership." He nodded. I continued. "Where are the truly effective leaders who will help create a better world? The present models of leadership don't seem to make a significant difference. The world is not getting any better. Where are the leaders of integrity, character, humility, effectiveness, and godliness? Why don't we talk about these things?"

And so began what was one of the most remarkable conversations I have ever had.

"I don't want to be offensive to you," I commented somewhat tentatively, "but would you allow me to talk about Jesus Christ?"

His response was quick, even vehement. "Jesus Christ? Why Jesus Christ? We're talking about leadership here, not about religion. Certainly not about Christianity."

"I'm not wanting to talk about religion, nor about Christianity," I replied. "But I believe that one of the greatest 'missed' lessons of history is found in the story of Jesus, that he was God's greatest, most dramatic and revolutionary model of leadership. Leadership, as God means it to be."

His answer was perceptive. "The Quran talks of Jesus as a great prophet. And yet he was executed as a common criminal. Surely you don't call that leadership. I don't see much of a model there. Is that success?"

Then, beginning in Luke 22, I explained to him the scriptural model of servant leadership as exemplified in the life of Jesus, that when the disciples were arguing among themselves as to who would be the greatest amongst them, Jesus had said, "The greatest among you should be like the youngest, and the one who rules like the one who serves. For who is greater, the one who is at the table or the one who serves? Is it not the one who is at the table? But I am among you as one who serves . . . and I confer on you a kingdom!" (Luke 22:26–29)

"What servant can possibly have a kingdom to bestow?" I asked. He was listening intently. "Obviously Jesus was dealing with a servanthood somewhat different from the understanding we have of the word within the context of our different cultures." He nodded. We agreed that "leading as a servant" would be the very antithesis of the dictatorial, power-oriented leadership so common in the world today. Jesus was addressing the failure of power-oriented leadership very clearly when he said to them, "You know that the rulers of the Gentiles lord it over them, and their high officials exercise authority over them. *Not so with you.* Instead, whoever wants to become great among you must be your servant, and whoever wants to be first must be your slave—just as the Son of Man did not come to be served, but to serve, and to give his life as a ransom for many" (Matthew 20:25–27, emphasis added).

Jesus modeled a leadership that is motivated by a desire to serve people and not to rule harshly over them. He was committed to seeking the good of those whom he led. His aim was to empower them, to put them first, even before himself. A servant-leader is one who works with strength and measurable effectiveness for the betterment of those he serves, and is not primarily motivated toward his own gain.

He looked somewhat puzzled, but clearly he was fascinated. We talked on. I again referred to the story in the Bible about the woman who was ambitious for her sons and requested of Jesus that they be chosen as the greatest among his disciples. His answer had been, "You don't know what you are asking." Jesus' style of leadership is different. It is revolutionary.

By this time I could see he was intrigued and stimulated. He asked me how such a leadership style could be transferable to the political world of today, where a leader's stature is more measured by power, status, and material success. How could it possibly work? There would be constant inner conflict, he believed, with man's innate sense of pride, his selfishness, his greed, and his lust for power. And in the political realm it would be worse. There would be no mercy there. "And, like

Jesus," he said, "such a leader would probably end up dead. And what good would that achieve? That would put an end to any leadership. Who wants to die?"

We discussed the profound paradox of death for a noble and godly cause, as opposed to life for a selfish or even evil cause.

We talked about the fact that, upon Jesus' death, his servant role was transferred to those who pledged to follow him. They may have stumbled. Some of them died as well! They may have failed—over and over again. But they were empowered with a godly wisdom. The world has been changed through servant leaders following Jesus. No other system of leadership has had such a profound influence for good.

I suggested that even for those consumed by the flawed standards of earthly leadership, the concept of leading from a serving position has an undeniable authenticity about it. Even to the most power-corrupted. "Take Mother Teresa, for example," I said. "A simple Albanian nun who gave her life that the poorest of India's poor might die with dignity. Measured against the accepted scale of materialism and power, Mother Teresa achieved little. And perhaps, in the eyes of some in the international political realm, she could never have been considered a leader. And yet the most prominent international leaders beat a path to her door and considered it an honor to be in her presence. From the world's most prestigious platforms, as well as from the gutters, she presented her message of servanthood. Like a shaft of light in the darkness, it was readily and warmly received. Why? Because servanthood in leadership is of God— and it has a ring of authenticity about it that is so appealing."

We agreed that this was Jesus' style of leadership. And that it could work. But it would be a brave person, a strong person, who could make such a change. It would take supernatural power.

We talked more about the death of Jesus, hanging naked on a Roman cross, for, on behalf of, and in the stead of those he came to lead. An ignominious defeat? No. A glorious victory. The apostle Paul spoke of this victory when he wrote about Jesus:

> *Who, being in very nature God,*
> *did not consider equality with God something to be grasped,*
> *but made himself nothing,*
> *taking the very nature of a servant, being made in human*
> *likeness.*
> *And being found in appearance as a man,*
> *he humbled himself and became obedient to death—*
> *even death on a cross!*
>
> PHILIPPIANS 2:6–8

We agreed that there was nowhere lower to go than that. It was servanthood in its most cogent expression. And yet, from this,

> *Therefore God exalted him to the highest place*
> *and gave him the name that is above every name,*
> *that at the name of Jesus every knee should bow,*
> *in heaven and on earth and under the earth,*
> *and every tongue confess that Jesus Christ is Lord,*
> *to the glory of God the Father.*
>
> PHILIPPIANS 2:9–11

Gone now was his brashness, the strident voice, and aggressive manner.

To my disappointment, however, at that time our host, the ambassador, called us all in to dinner. We were placed at different tables—and the conversation ended.

Until midnight.

After a most enjoyable evening of friendship and hospitality, it was time to go. My MAF colleague and I made our way down into the underground car-park. As we stepped out of the elevator into a poorly lit area a dim figure was waiting in the darkness. It was the man with whom I had conversed for so long before dinner.

He approached us. "I didn't want to talk with you again with so many people around," he said, "so I have been waiting for you here. I have something to ask of you."

I was somewhat taken aback.

"Could you in any way extend your stay in this nation? Twenty-four hours would be wonderful. Longer, if possible. Please tell no one. I would like to arrange for you to come away with me where we can talk with openness, with no possibility of interruption. I would love to talk more with you about Jesus, about the concept you opened up to me of his model for leadership and servanthood."

The truth, the incisive wisdom of God's Word, had broken through. There was a longing to know more.

In that country the door that in many ways was beginning to close for some of my mission friends, was opening to us. Indeed it was opened personally by the president of the nation—and we had been welcomed as we entered.

When I recounted this story to a friend, he commented, "You have a lot of gall saying stuff like that to such people. These are significant leaders. They are trained, experienced in the cut and thrust of national and international affairs. Talk of a 'Gentle Jesus, meek and mild' flies in the face of what the world says about strength in leadership. Following Jesus' style! It may work in the church, but in the political and corporate world of today, it's unthinkable that the concept of servant leadership would work."

True?

We people of God must confirm that if God's Word is not just true, but truth—absolute truth; if it is all that we need for life—then what it says about leadership is authentic, viable, and relevant in every arena of our lives. What it teaches is not merely the leadership "flavor of the month" or another alternative. It is truth. Absolute truth.

In the Gospels it is not recorded that Jesus taught his disciples anything about leadership! He taught almost exclusively about following. Why? Perhaps it was because one simply cannot be a leader unless he or she has a full understanding of what it means to follow. And that is perhaps the first great lesson about leadership.

Jesus *modeled* leadership rather than taught it.

Jesus was always pointing us back to the stories of his Father's dealings with his people. Scattered throughout the Bible are the lessons of godly leadership, principles that if followed by the leaders of today, or any age, would bring peace, contentment, and success.

In ancient times, Joseph was the master of Potiphar's household. But as a servant. I doubt that he ever shook his fist at Potiphar or tried to control him. He simply served. He did his job well. And he was given authority over his household.

The Bible doesn't only speak of servant-leadership, of course. It deals with leadership across its broadest spectrum. It deals very clearly with the responsibility of leaders to empower, to shepherd, to encourage, to relate personally, to pastor, to be strong. But primarily, to be servants.

Servant leadership works. It must. It's designed by God.

Chapter

14

IRON AND CLAY

Of all the church leaders I have known over the years, there was one with whom I had a particular difficulty, against whom I even harbored a degree of resentment. And I have felt guilty about it ever since.

It wasn't even that I knew him well or had personally worked with him on a daily basis. He was a leader in an African country, and I lived in the U.S. But I heard his name frequently. It seemed, somehow, he was always creating burdens and even barriers for our already overburdened staff and standing in the way of great opportunity. There were exciting things happening in his nation, things in which MAF was privileged to be a significant part. Yet this man always seemed to be playing politics and using his position in a way that made things more complicated for us. I saw him as a power-oriented leader.

There was a time, I knew, when he had been different. His path to leadership was not atypical of the development of many national leaders coming out of the colonial "mission" era. His potential had been obvious to the Western missionaries who worked in his area and through whose efforts the church had been brought to birth. They singled him out when he was quite young, guiding his education and personal development. They made expansive promises to him—of prominent schools in America and Europe, post-graduate degrees, an American doctorate. And most of these promises were fulfilled.

He had been a very gifted young man with natural leadership potential. Over and over this was reinforced in his mind. He knew that the process through which he was being guided was to prepare him for much bigger things in the "post-missionary" life of the church in his nation. And he also knew that the same process could lead him into a position of significant power.

Thus, as the foreign missionary influence decreased, his influence increased—as did his ambition, his pride in himself, and his powerful stand against anyone who stood in his way.

Through times of horrendous heartache, stress, and danger, this nation had gradually developed in its independence. Thousands of lives were lost as rival factions and ethnic groups struggled for supremacy. The nation that emerged was in the control of people whose hands were bloodied. Power was absolute. Opposition was dealt with swiftly, and with an iron fist.

And the church stood through all those years of struggle. It didn't just stand—it grew and thrived. The church was alive. It was vigorous and enthusiastic. All over the nation, groups of believers, many of them poor villagers struggling for survival, found great hope and comfort in their relationship with God. This was no foreign church transplanted from the West. It was indigenous, with national character and cultural distinctives. And it was on the move. It knew rich and deep joy in the face of terrible opposition.

But among the many restrictions placed upon the church by the despotic president of the nation was an edict that denominational identity had to be yielded to an enforced categorization dictated by him. All the different mission and church groups served by MAF found themselves member organizations of one national body, a heterogeneous collection of major denominations whose spectrum of theological identity was extremely broad.

And this gifted young man of such great promise and potential became its leader. He then proclaimed himself "bishop-for-life." As a personal friend of the president, and as one who was himself extremely ambitious, he had now acquired great status and power.

Henri Nouwen talks of this lifestyle as the way of the world. "Be relevant, do something spectacular, accept world power." But Nouwen goes on to say that

> Jesus rejects this option and chooses God's way, a way of humility revealing itself gradually to be the way of the cross.
>
> It is hard to accept that God would reveal his divine presence to us in the self-emptying, humble way of the man of Nazareth. So much in me seeks influence, power, success, and popularity. But the way of Jesus is the way of hiddenness, powerlessness, and littleness. It does not seem a very appealing way. Yet when I enter into true, deep communion with Jesus I will find that it is the way that leads to real joy and peace.*

As the years went by, the integrity level of this church leader, perhaps predictably, seemed to diminish. Increasingly, I

*Henri Nouwen, *The Road to Daybreak* (New York: Doubleday).

saw him as an obstacle, a challenge, even an adversary. His closeness to the president of the nation and his apparent wealth in a country of devastatingly poor people, disturbed me. He was a leader to be reckoned with, a formidable foe to any who disagreed with him or opposed his actions.

But I had heard stories of another side of this man, of changes that had taken place in his spirit at a major Congress on Evangelism in Europe. An older missionary related to me how this now prominent church figure had returned home with a passion for evangelism and a warm, genuine concern for the souls of his countrymen. And for a time things were different. He preached often at large gatherings in the city and in rural areas. For some who had seen him previously standing in the way of true growth and progress in the church, there seemed to be new hope. Their leader again had a heart for the lost, a heart for his people as a whole.

But the enticement of political recognition and addiction to the power of the old leadership style didn't really go away.

One man used the picture in the vision given to Daniel, that young leader of Old Testament days, comparing him to ". . . an enormous, dazzling statue, awesome in appearance. The head of the statue was made of pure gold, its chest and arms of silver, its belly and thighs of bronze, its legs of iron, its feet partly of iron and partly of baked clay" (Daniel 2:31–33).

"In those days he was just like the feet of that statue," my friend said. "There was some iron there, some real strength and solidarity, but it was all mixed up with clay."

To my shame, I never saw the iron. Only the clay!

On one occasion, when we were planning to re-deploy some of our many aircraft in that nation, he sent a message to me. "You can do what you like with MAF aircraft and resources in any other place," he said. "That's your right. But here in this country, MAF belongs to me!"

Belongs to him?

This required immediate response. Within a few days I was in his office with our manager and a few of his personal advisors. The atmosphere was tense. In spite of his fluency in English, he insisted on using French. He began by delivering a diatribe of condemnation, firstly of MAF, then expanding to all other foreign work being carried out in his country. "I will say what you do here. Airplanes you bring into this country are to be used only as directed by me. I reject your right to make the changes you are considering. I reject your claim to ownership of any assets in this land. They belong to me. I reject your Western, foreign methods of service. I can see through to the real motivation of your plan. It is just a power-play for your own growth and development."

Swaying back in his chair, as his interpreter translated his words to me into English, he went on to label "mission" as racist, self-serving, and evil. He spoke about colonial greed, saying accusingly that everything ever done in his nation had been patronizing and motivated by power. All Westerners, he said, missionaries included, sought to exert control over people considered "lesser brethren." It was his God-given task to oppose them.

Suddenly my mind flashed back to the conversation about political leadership I had had with the Islamic leader some years before, about power-oriented leadership, about manipulation for personal greed. What this church leader was saying was a mirror-image of these same concepts, but in this case, directed at church/mission leadership. Did he really see us like that?

Yet at the same time, as a Christian himself, he was clearly demonstrating to me the identical attributes of a leadership flawed by a desire for personal power and self-aggrandizement.

For almost an hour he continued to harangue us.

As he made these accusations with such strength, he looked around at the staff he had gathered together. They remained silent. This was not just a confrontation with the leader of an American organization. This was a message to them, his pastors and church leaders. His authority was not to be questioned or threatened in any way.

He was bishop for life!

I only saw him once more—many years later—in that same office. I had not been summoned there, nor did I have any agenda other than to pay him a courtesy call. I had phoned and had been given an appointment mid-morning on a certain weekday. But when I arrived at his office his secretary was most apologetic and explained that it would be impossible for me to see the bishop on that day. "His sister has just died this morning. They were very, very close. He is in his office, packing. He is heartbroken. He is leaving soon to collect her body and take it back home for burial," she said.

I asked for one minute, not to intrude, but just to pray with him.

As I entered his office he was putting his clerical vestments into a case. I explained to him that I had no business to discuss, but that hearing of his sister's passing, I simply wanted to extend to him our loving sympathy—and to pray with him. And so I prayed—a simple prayer—for him. I asked God to give him grace to minister to his wider family back home, that divine love would flow through him to bring comfort to the bereaved, and that he would be used by God in that very difficult and emotional situation.

He asked me to stay for awhile. He had tea served. We talked for about an hour. We didn't talk about MAF. We didn't talk about colonialism. We didn't talk about racism or about power or about hatred. We talked about God, about life, about death, and about eternity. We talked about grace.

As brothers in Christ together, we spoke. It was a precious time. We acknowledged our individual weaknesses, our faltering baby-steps of faith, and our deep need of the daily empowering of the Holy Spirit. We confessed to each other our pride, our self-serving, our propensity to "think more highly of ourselves than we ought to think."

He cried as he talked about his sister.

Finally I asked, "If you could choose where you might live, what you might do, and whom you might work with, what would be your choice?" His answer came from the depth of his heart. It came from his very soul.

"I would just like to be back in the village as a simple pastor," he said, sobbing. "I would like a simple life. I would like to be done with this place of power and pressure. I would like to be where I could love people for Jesus' sake. What is more important, I would like to be somewhere where people would love me!"

As if for the first time, I saw through and beneath his power. Strangely enough, I pictured a butterfly, and its emergence from a very unattractive cocoon. But in him the picture was somehow reversed. Something beautiful, something with marvelous potential to give pleasure, to minister love, had been progressively bound up and enslaved by the threads of corruption and greed, until the bright colors and useful wings were now almost completely covered in this dark, opaque cocoon.

I saw beyond the clay of Daniel's vision to the iron, to the real, authentic strength of the man. I saw in his soul a longing to reject all the "stuff" that he had allowed to allure and trap him into being what most people saw him to be, something and someone they and he didn't like.

I felt chastened. I had never thought positively about him. Not once. I had not really even tried to find any good in him. He had been little more than an adversary to me, a man corrupted by power, a despotic, self-serving leader. I had never seen beneath that complex surface, and had therefore never found the simple, plain man who longed to walk humbly with God and with his people.

Leadership. So easily corrupted. So often criticized. So sadly neglected.

As I have traveled on every continent and in scores of countries in recent years, I have developed a strong conviction that one of this generation's greatest challenges is in the area of leadership. "Where are the world's great leaders of today?" is the cry in the field of politics, government, business—and in the church as well.

But leadership is changing. The leadership gurus of our day are continually redefining its qualities and style. Hierarchy is out! That strong, firm, militaristic, "top-down" approach, so widespread particularly in the days of colonialism now belongs to yesteryear. Team, Group, Trust, Shared, Empowerment, Facilitator, Shepherd, Servant are the words of today's generation.

Sounds familiar to a reader of the Bible, doesn't it?

In the so-called sophistication of the West, the corporate world leads. It certainly leads the church! See how young are some of the most prominent of today's business leaders. And so many of them are women. But in the non-Western world, the world where developing nations struggle in their earnest search for recognition and dignity in independence, the model left for them by colonial masters falls far short. In addition, cultural traits, ethnicity, and tribalism do not always impact the growth to maturity in a positive way. Thus, we often see a totally unworkable, adversarial, and unsuccessful leadership desperately crying for help.

From our lofty and often patronizing positions of paternalism and pride, we stand apart. And we criticize. Without a second thought, we use words like graft, corruption, greed, power, selfish, non-caring, hopeless. We see no workable solution to the leadership problems in these smaller, poorer, struggling nations.

We gave to that world our systems of government, pressing those same systems upon their completely different cultures. We left them our models of leadership. We built our righteous ramparts, we scaled these walls and trampled, like crusaders. We march on, often oblivious to the wounded spirits we left behind. Yet now we are so quick to judge—often without understanding or with only limited knowledge. We seldom look deeper than the things that concern us and we form negative opinions without offering the justice that we would want for ourselves. We don't stop to think what hurting heart might lie behind the ugly barriers and high walls that people build around themselves. It doesn't even cross our minds that there might be a troubled, captive soul in there, longing to be released, trying to break down those walls from the inside but not having the strength to do so and desperately crying out for God.

Leadership. It's a tough task. Readily criticized. Often so lonely.

I urge, then, first of all, that requests, prayers, intercession and thanksgiving be made for everyone—for kings and all those in authority, that we may live peaceful and quiet lives in all godliness and holiness.

1 TIMOTHY 2:1–2

Chapter

15

TEAM LEADER

One Friday afternoon Jo and I stopped in Chicago on the way home from an overseas trip. Our youngest son, Chris, and his wife Elizabeth were studying there, living not far from the downtown area in a small apartment. We checked into a nearby hotel and made plans to take them out to dinner and have the weekend together.

"Do you know what I'd like to do?" Jo asked, as she lay back on the hotel bed. "I'd love to hear the Chicago Symphony Orchestra. Tonight. With Daniel Barenboim conducting. Wouldn't it be an incredible coincidence if they just happened to be performing—and we could get four seats?" she said.

Amazingly, that's just what happened. The fortunate timing of my call at the very moment a subscriber phoned to cancel his regular center-front box reservation, found us, two hours later, being ushered into the finest seats of Chicago's downtown concert hall. It seemed we could almost reach out and touch the stage.

It was a sold-out concert.

As usual, there didn't seem to be much order to the entry of the orchestra. The members filtered in one at a time, found their seats, and sat down. They talked a little to one another, arranged the music on their stands, and got ready to play. They seemed oblivious to the thousands who sat before them in the audience waiting with eager anticipation for the music to begin.

A flautist executed a few scales. Up and down. A trumpeter blew an arpeggio or two. The timpanist tuned his drums, lightly tapping each of them, his head low over the drum skin to get the exact pitch. A variety of stringed instruments began to tune up. Violins. Violas. Cellos. Basses.

Soon everyone was playing. More than a hundred performers. But it was not a pretty sound. In fact it was pretty awful! A cacophony of competing noises. And it seemed like a competition. I thought of the Scripture verse (Deuteronomy 12:8): Everyone did what was right in their own eyes.

Chris put his fingers in his ears and looked at me with raised eyebrows, his body language asking, "Why did you bring me to this?"

The oboist played a single note, setting the pitch. First one instrument played, then another, as each instrument was finely tuned.

After a few minutes, the noise lessened. Suddenly, all was quiet.

To a thunderous ovation, Daniel Barenboim entered and walked to center stage. He bowed to the audience. He turned to adjust the music on his lectern. The applause tapered off. Then, with arms raised, he stood before his orchestra. There was total silence!

All those musicians. One leader. Absolute attention and concentration.

With a rhythmic, smooth movement of his arms—indeed his entire body—Barenboim commenced to lead his orchestra into the wonder and delight of the music they had prepared for us.

What a transformation!

Discord was gone. Competition was replaced by absolute harmony. And from that stage, as if with a single voice, rose the beauty of the finest music, produced in marvelous accord. With wonder we listened, our emotions captured by the feast of rhythm and melody, harmony, and cadence.

There was giving. There was taking. There was sharing. There was leading. There was following. But always, together-ness. It seemed as if no mere human could have composed such beautiful sound. Sometimes there was opportunity for individual instruments to demonstrate their uniqueness. At times the orchestra played as one, so quietly it didn't seem possible that they were indeed all playing together. The conductor interpreted constantly, with his graceful body language and skillful hand movements, every nuance, every mood, every emotion of the composer's brilliance. At times, with the crashing of cymbals, the blaring of brass, and the smashing of drums the entire orchestra poured out a thrilling crescendo of spine-tingling sound.

What a concert!

During the intermission, Maestro Barenboim actually sat on the floor of the stage with his feet dangling over the edge and just talked with the people. He answered their questions and explained the music. It was a family concert. It had been organized specifically to introduce those who did not usually make a practice of listening to classical music to the excitement of a symphony orchestra.

I loved the way he handled a question about rock music. There was no scorn. No criticism. In fact there was an open and very genuine recognition that the music of rock and roll has its own special valuable place in the world of entertainment. He applauded the skill and professionalism of exponents of this different art form. Daniel Barenboim is not just a world-class musician, a renowned maestro. He is a very capable communicator.

The audience loved him.

We took a break after his informal chat with the audience. We stood sipping drinks in the crowded mezzanine. There was a buzz of conversation—much adulation for Barenboim, the orchestra, the glory of the music, and the enjoyment of the night.

What a treat. To have seats in the central box of that wonderful concert hall, to hear one of the world's finest orchestras under the baton of one of the world's leading conductors. We were so close it seemed we could almost reach out and touch the shiny bald spot on the back of his head. It was a night to remember.

As the final notes of the last piece on the program died away, the audience of that full house stood to its feet in a standing ovation. On and on, we clapped our appreciation.

Barenboim acknowledged the thunderous applause with grace. He bowed respectfully. But then, in what seemed to me a humble way, he directed the audience's applause to every member of the orchestra. First, the concertmaster. Then, in turn, each of those who had taken solo parts in a number of places stood to take his or her bow, graciously acknowledging the honor given by the maestro. Everybody was applauded. Each musician was afforded a gracious recognition by the leader.

Honor deserved. Honor generously given.

On the way back to the apartment, Chris made some fascinating comments. He said, "You know, when the orchestra was tuning up, it sounded awful. It was like a horrible competition. I really didn't think I was going to enjoy it at all. But when the conductor had their total concentration," he continued, "and the music began, it seemed as if all those competing individuals became one. From where we were sitting, looking down on the stage, I couldn't help thinking that the orchestra resembled a huge black and white creature that suddenly came to life. And it had the most amazing voice!"

What a powerful lesson about leadership.

Had Daniel Barenboim not directed the applause to his musicians—every last one of them—the ovation, nevertheless, would still have been given to him. It was his by right. But he didn't take it all for himself. It was with genuine recognition of a wonderful performance on the part of the entire orchestra that he drew the audience's attention to every single individual member of his musical family.

I wonder what would have happened if each musician had sought to be heard above everyone else, if the concert had become a battlefield of persons wanting to excel alone, wanting to show off. What would that have sounded like? I think the maestro would have packed up and gone home in disgust—leaving the conglomeration of discordant players to fight it out.

The orchestra played inspiring music that night. Was it played Barenboim's way? Yes. As the leader it was his right and responsibility to interpret the works of the composer. But he trusted each member to play the notes exactly the way that the composer had written them and, at the same time, to follow his interpretation, his—the conductor's—leading.

And he shared the credit that he so richly deserved with each of his musicians.

Jethro, Moses' father-in-law, saw that his son-in-law was living under an intolerable burden of leadership. So he drew up a plan to relieve Moses of the stress and strain. As recorded in Exodus 18, he directed Moses:

> Select capable men from all the people . . . and appoint them as officials over thousands, hundreds, fifties and tens. Have them serve as judges for the people at all times, but have them bring every difficult case to you; the simple cases they can decide themselves. That will make your load lighter. . . . If you do this and God so commands, you will be able to stand the strain, and all these people will go home satisfied."

"If God commands"? But God didn't command.

What God eventually commanded was similar, but with one significant difference. In Numbers 11, when Moses was totally overburdened with his leadership responsibility, he pleaded with God, "I cannot carry all these people by myself; the burden is too heavy for me. If this is how you are going to treat me, put me to death right now."

Apparently Jethro's plan was not working. Then God revealed his design for leadership. And it was significantly different.

> Bring me seventy of Israel's elders who are known to you as Israel's leaders and officials among the people. Have them come to the Tent of Meeting, that they may stand there with you. I will come down and speak with you there, and I will take of the Spirit that is on you, and put the Spirit on them. They will help you carry the burden of the people so that you will not have to carry it alone.

Take of his leadership spirit . . . and put it on them?

The difference is in empowerment, in the sharing of the Spirit. Moses was still the leader but the Spirit was shared with those he led. Thus we see that leadership is a team effort. The Spirit and the credit—is shared.

Empowerment. An integral part of leadership. Jesus empowers his followers to do the work his Father assigned him. And he shares the glory that is rightfully his with those who follow him.

What leadership! And what a symphony!

It is a symphony of incredible grace ...

of unfailing love ...

of radical life changes ...

of exciting and eternal promises.

And in the grandest statement of humility the world has ever seen, God, the great Maestro, stepped down from heaven, walked and talked with us, and showed us how to make the music of heaven.

Now people everywhere, the educated and the simple, the wealthy and the poor, the influential and the anonymous people from every nation, tribe, and tongue, every day and every hour around the planet, are playing his symphony.

And the Lord shares the glory of it all, his glory, with us.

In order that we may also share in his glory.

ROMANS 8:17

FOUNDATIONS

"I don't know where it is, Michael, but it must be somewhere near here."

We were forcing our way through tropical growth between the road from the beach, about thirty yards away. It grabbed at our sweaty skin and our clothes. The ground underfoot was wet and soft. Vines, creepers, and succulent plants surrounded us, up to six or seven feet high. The brilliant sapphire-colored sea, just beyond the low sandy dunes, was mirror-like, visible through the undergrowth and tall coconut palms. Although the sea was calm, like shiny, rich blue glass, tiny waves made soft swishing sounds as they broke lazily upon the gray sand.

It was so hot. So humid. So very—Wewak.

At that latitude, almost on the equator, the sun shines fiercely from directly overhead. Nothing alleviated the heavy pall of tropical heat and humidity that dragged the sweat out of our bodies in balls upon our foreheads and in rivulets down our backs.

This was August 2000, and my eldest son, Michael, and I were trying to find the place where our house had stood when we first came to Papua New Guinea in 1961. We had just flown in from Mount Hagen and decided to look for our old home before we did anything else. We crossed the road between the airstrip and the small settlement of national houses scattered around the area where our house had been.

"Everything looks so small after thirty years, Dad," Michael remarked in a surprised voice. "I guess I was just a little kid then."

The house was no longer standing. We hadn't expected to find it, anyway. But the foundation, a two-foot-thick cement slab, should surely be there, somewhere.

Two or three men and a woman stood watching us. Obviously they wondered what on earth two white strangers were doing poking around their village and trying to force a way into the heavy bushes nearby.

We used the old airfield hangar as a reference point, but uncurbed tropical growth had totally changed the landscape. Nothing was recognizable. Eventually, behind a yellow-painted wooden trade store building, we found a single old cement slab. At one time it had obviously been the foundation of something. *"Mi harim tok, bipo dispela em i haus bilong ol contrak,"* one of the men said. ("I've heard that long ago this was a house for plantation contract workers.")

In 1961 there had been an ex-World War II Quonset hut where primitive bushmen from distant areas were accommodated. They had been recruited to work in the copra plantations on the outer islands of Papua New Guinea. Sometimes they stayed for weeks in Wewak, waiting for a chartered DC3 to take them to their destinations. Most of them had never seen a car, a road, the sea—and certainly not a white woman.

This was our answer. It was the clue we needed.

This dome-shaped corrugated metal hut had been barely fifty feet from our house.

"That means that the foundation of our place must be in the middle of that heavy stuff over there," we said to each other as we launched off into the even thicker undergrowth.

And there it was!

Hidden inside a dense mass of bushes, creepers, and vines was the clear outline of a building. It was obviously the old cement slab. But now it was a dense mass, about twelve inches deep, of succulent leaves. Creepers and vines of all sorts completely covered it. They had gradually enveloped it as the years had passed. All signs of the structure had long since gone. But not the foundation!

It was the floor-plan of our house, without a doubt. In rich, verdant green.

I scrambled up onto the slab and stood there remembering.

Thirty nine years, almost to the day, slipped away. I was walking into the house for the first time, with Jo and seventeen-month-old Michael. We had been driven a number of miles out of the small town of Wewak along a dusty road in MAF's World War II jeep. "No other white people live out here," we were told. I had tried not to show my shock and horror when I saw where we would be living. Little more than a shed, unlined and constructed of thin, heat-attracting silver aluminum. Partitions of the same material formed a main bedroom barely large enough for the double bed. There were two even smaller bedrooms, one containing a single bed and the other, a "meat-safe" cot.

The house had no regular windows. Each room had one four-foot length of the exterior cladding, hinged at the top, that could be propped open with a stick. But no fly-wire to stop the invading hordes of anopheles mosquitoes, all ready and waiting to share the malaria they carried. The roof was formed of sheets of this Kingstrand aluminum. These were held together with rows of small bolts and nuts that in the extreme heat of midday would "pop" right out. When the first inevitable rainstorms came later that night, we realized that we were living in something resembling a giant, upturned colander.

Wall-to-wall carpet was very fashionable in those days. We had wall-to-wall malthoid, a building material composed of pitch-impregnated paper. Someone had thoughtfully laid it over the rough cement to which it had firmly attached itself. Within a few moments of our arrival that first day, our white-skinned Michael in his white, cloth diapers, resembled a Dalmatian. We found to our dismay that the tar melted in the heat and adhered permanently to feet, shoes, clothes, and anything else that came in contact with it. We tried many times to remove that charming black wall-to-wall floor covering. Unsuccessfully. It's probably still there, under the updated carpet of green leaves.

The side entrance to the house was via an upturned wooden crate. There was no electricity. It was miles from town. No other white people lived so far out.

What a dwelling place! Why, then, were Michael and I so anxious to find where it had been? Why? Because the fifteen months we'd spent there had indelibly printed upon our minds the most amazing and unique memories. Humorous and hilarious, horrible and hard, hazardous and humiliating—but above all, happy, happy memories.

I stepped onto what had been the floor of our tiny kitchen. I pictured my beautiful, young, six-months-pregnant wife, fresh from her comfortable, upper-class home in Adelaide as she struggled to cook on a two-burner, kerosene "wick" stove. Often it refused to light. Mostly it went out almost immediately, anyway. There was no oven. We didn't need one. The whole house was a giant oven!

I walked over to where the living area had been. It doubled as a dining room, barely large enough for the long table with a bench down each side. I remembered the meals we ate there in the light of our one pressure lamp, and vividly recalled the intense pain of the third-degree burns I received to my arm when the lamp exploded as I was lighting it three days after our arrival. I had to hitch a ride to the Wewak hospital in the town's one and only taxi that, miraculously, was passing by right at that time. We didn't even know the town had a taxi! Jo and Michael were left alone in pitch darkness.

Moving a few feet, I stood where our double bed had been. Memories came tumbling into my mind.

—The six-foot-long snake we discovered in the beam of our flashlight that first night. It had taken up residence on top of the aluminum wall above the bed.

—Jo opting to walk along the dark road to a distant house for help while I babysat the reptile. We had absolutely no idea what to do. Many were the subsequent stories about the new MAF pilot who couldn't even kill a snake.

—Sitting on the bed with guests, crammed together under the enormous superfine mosquito net, eating dinner, playing cards, laughing uproariously, and drawing straws to see who would brave the sandfly and mosquito hordes to go make a cup of tea! After dusk, inside the net on the double bed was the only bug-free haven we had.

—Lying in bed listening to the roaring of the surf crashing on the beach a few yards away, and hearing the reverberations as violent tropical thunderstorms rattled the entire house and lightning illuminated the silver walls.

—Trying to decide whether to close the shutters against the driving rain and stifle, or open them and get wet.

—Tending to Tim, our tiny, sickly baby born in January 1962, whose little crib stood in the makeshift wardrobe in the corner of the room. Wardrobe? It was merely a piece of three-by-three plywood suspended from the ceiling. There was a broom handle from one corner to the other where we normally hung our clothes. That is, when Tim wasn't using it as his personal shelter! It effectively kept the drips off him whenever it rained.

I took a few more paces to where Michael's small bedroom had been and remembered the horror we felt on the morning we discovered that during the night rats had gnawed every casein button off his pajama top. There was disgust mixed with amusement on another morning when we found him pushing his little toy boat around the bedroom in three inches of water. He had loaded it with "cargo," he told us. The long brown object in it had floated in with the king tide during the night. The transit contract workers who lived in the Quonset hut next door had no toilet facilities except the bushes. Anything deposited there was flushed out in the gently swirling waters and frequently floated into our house through the spaces under the doors and walls. Our slab, of course, was at ground level. On an exceptionally high tide or in a big storm, there was no escaping the water that flowed over the sand hill and into our small depression. Sometimes it was two-feet deep in the yard . . . and six inches deep throughout the house.

Nearby national houses were built on stilts, their floors well above water level. This also made them much more comfortable. They caught even the slightest breeze from the ocean. We, on the other hand, were denied this luxury in our hot little hollow.

Michael and I stepped across to stand on the shape of the old front porch. The slab is lower there, where the ground slopes upward a few feet to the road. We saw an enormous frangipani tree just to the right. It overhangs the road and is covered with fragrant pink and white blossoms. "We planted that," I exclaimed to Michael with surprise and delight. "It was just a scraggy, two-foot-long shoot when we stuck it in the ground." I wondered whether Jo's red salvia plants were still growing. She had planted them outside the front door. They were brilliantly colorful after a good rain. The rest of the time they were gray-green, as was everything else in the vicinity, including the contents of the house. Clouds of pervasive white crushed coral dust from the road a few feet away filled the air with each passing vehicle. But I saw no red salvia in the dense bush.

A power pole still stood there. I wondered if it was the same one that had been erected all those years ago. I relived the excitement of that memorable day. We had been without electricity for more than six months, but finally the power was on! A heavy black cable, like a huge umbilical cord, was fed through the gap between the wall and the roof. It was suspended across the middle of the "living" room and anchored on the far wall. We attached to it a proliferation of double adapters, one upon the other, like some grotesque tree! Extension cords snaked all over the house. We had light. We had power for a fry-pan. We had fans! Luxury living—provided there was no power failure.

But there is a downside to everything. The prolific, large gray rats in the area, who insisted on sharing our house, found the long, hanging wire a marvelous place to perform their tightrope walking skills, especially after dark. I can still hear the terrified shriek of an overnight guest whom we had neglected to inform about our furry friends. "Yikes!" she screamed at about 1:00 A.M. when she encountered a troupe of them practicing their balancing act on the high wire. In the light of her flashlight, their glaring beady eyes seemed to say, "How dare you invade our domain." And all she had wanted was a drink of water.

Finally I turned and trod my way over the carpet of thick vines to the back of the foundation and stood on the very edge. I looked out across the Bismark Sea.

I saw myself a young man again, eagerly kissing my small family good-bye and excitedly leaving to go and fly. To live my dreams. To do what I had known since I was a teenager God had called me to do with my life. For a few moments I stood there quietly.

And then, in my imagination, I see her. Clearly. Now on her own for the day. A slim, tanned young mother, still with her mop of curly blonde hair. She hauls the heavy baby carriage across the creeper-covered dune and drags it through the already hot, soft sand of the beach. A little boy races ahead. His sturdy brown legs are covered with scars and infected sores from multiple mosquito and sand fly bites. They reach the water's edge.

And there she sits, hour after hour, day after endless day, in the shallow, tepid water. Even the continual irritation of sand midges is preferable to the intolerable heat of the metal house in the hollow behind her.

From time to time she takes her frail, fretful baby from his net-enshrouded carriage and nurses him. She has made a simple shelter from the sun for him, using long sticks and a large beach towel. The toddler splashes and plays in the water. "Perhaps he'll be happy for awhile," she thinks hopefully.

Some distance away a group of brown-skinned children are swimming. Their faint chatter and laughter drift back to her over the long stretch of gray-white sand. A solitary man fishes nearby with a long pole fashioned from the center rib of a sago palm frond. The shore is littered with flotsam and jetsam. Driftwood. Washed in on the last tide. She sees the branch of a small tree. *I wonder how far that has come,* she thinks. *I wonder what sort of tree it once was.*

The branch has been bleached by the sun, scoured by the sand, washed and scrubbed clean by the tumbling, salty waves. It has no bark, no leaves, no buds, no flowers. It is the bare white skeleton of what was once part of a beautiful tree.

That's just how I feel, she thinks, as she looks at the stark, bare, white branches. *Abandoned, lonely, useless, washed up on an isolated beach. The things that were so precious to me are mostly gone. My friends and family. My career. My music. The comforts of my home. Even my own personal ministry.*

Silent tears roll down her cheeks.

"God," she cries out in her heart. "Where are you? Is this all my missionary service is going to be? Is this why you brought me to this land so far from home?"

And she weeps and weeps.

No one sees. No one knows.

Except God. And he puts his loving arms around her and comforts her.

———

Jo never let me see the tears she shed there on that lonely beach or in that stifling hot aluminum house. Many years went by before I even heard this story. She was sharing it then with some MAF women.

I write this as a tribute to her courage.

And to the courage of all those other women, her much loved friends, the wives of my colleagues in MAF.

The old house is gone. But the foundations remain. The memories too. They will never be taken away.

———

I'm reminded of another foundation.

For years we worked there in that Sepik district of Papua New Guinea. Every morning the quietness and tranquillity of that scene would be shattered by the howling of Cessna engines as we took off to fly out across the mountains.

It was truly a missionary endeavor. People brought a multiplicity of skills and gifts to be used in a joint strategy of evangelism, church planting, and holistic development. Those we served were not exclusively evangelists and preachers by a long shot. Medical doctors, nurses, teachers, agriculturists, builders, linguists, anthropologists—all were included.

But there was a preponderance of white in that brown country.

More than thirty years later I revisited one of the former major areas of mission activity. In the earlier years, perhaps twenty-five white-skinned men and women would have joyfully welcomed the plane's arrival. But this time, as we landed, there was not a white face to be seen. Everything looked the same. The familiar buildings were still there. I remembered carrying in most of that roofing metal myself in my Cessna 180.

But now it was all brown. There were hundreds of happily smiling national people, eager to shake my hand and greet me on that day.

I had a marvelous conversation with the leader of the church, a man whom I had first met when he was a young Bible college student. I had expected to find that, with the departure of all the missionaries, church numbers would have dwindled. But I was thrilled as he told me a far different story. "There are eighty-five thousand believers in this area," he said, beaming at me. "There is great enthusiasm and life in the church."

"Well, then, how do you now look back on the days when there were so many white missionaries here?" I asked him. His answer thrilled me even more. It affirmed again to me how abundantly worthwhile had been my thirty-seven years in MAF.

"How do I view those days?" He paused a moment. "Let me say just two things," he continued, in his very adequate English. "Firstly, we wouldn't be here as a church if you had not come. Nor would we have been so strong as a people. Yes, as you say, there were a lot of white skins in those days. We did feel put upon sometimes. We had difficulties dealing with the emergence into the twentieth century. But we thank God for you all, for your coming."

"Secondly," he said, "looking back at the situation as it was then and comparing it to what it is today, I would say this—

God used you and our other mission friends to lay a foundation that was to be the basis for his future work. It was on the foundation you laid that God later built the church we have here today!"

Foundations!

I flew away that day with a renewed understanding of the purpose of so much of our service. And a deep thankfulness as I realized in a fresh way the inestimable privilege of being a "foundation builder."

That old cement foundation Michael and I so recently walked upon eloquently retold and vividly brought to mind precious personal memories. Yes, the house is gone. But the foundation is standing the test of time. Perhaps someone, some day, will bulldoze it away. It probably won't last forever.

But our memories, and the things we learned in the months we lived there, will last for all time. And that, we now see, was God's divine purpose for our lives.

We learned about courage, tenacity, and commitment. We learned as well the need for humor and joy. We learned much about the importance of supportive friends and family, about faith, about caring for and loving one another in a new way. And, oh, how much we learned about prayer! But mostly we learned about God and his faithfulness. "I will never leave you or forsake you," he said to us over and over again.

This was the foundation he built *into us* during that time, the qualities and strengths he knew we needed for the years ahead.

Yes, this personal foundation has been buffeted by huge storms. Sometimes it has been submerged by "king tides." Its very base has even been threatened with destruction. But it has withstood the test of time. And it still stands today.

And what of that other foundation? The kingdom foundation we were privileged to build? That, especially, will never pass away. Never! No bulldozer can remove it. No one will ever have to force his way through thick jungle to find it. For that foundation, and the house built upon it—the church—will always stand.

Not even the gates of hell shall prevail against it.

The Builder promised that!

For no one can lay any foundation other than the one already laid, which is Jesus Christ.

1 CORINTHIANS 3:11

MISSION AVIATION FELLOWSHIP

Mission Aviation Fellowship was formed soon after World War II to impact the world of mission, to bring development to the isolated and the poor, and to bring relief to the suffering through the use of aviation technology. MAF exists to "multiply the effectiveness of the church" as it reaches out with the Good News of the Gospel of Jesus Christ. In recent years, various aspects of Information Technology have been added to expand MAF's effectiveness even more.

Working in more than 35 countries around the world, MAF has utilized an aircraft fleet of more than 150 airplanes.

If you would like more information about MAF, contact:

MAF-USA:
P.O. Box 3202
Redlands, CA USA 92373-0998

MAF-Australia:
P.O. Box 211
Box Hill, Vic. 3128 Australia

MAF-Europe:
Focus House
Godington Road
Ashford, Kent. TN23 1HA
United Kingdom

MAF-Canada:
P.O. Box 368
Guelph, Ont. N1H 6K5
Canada

Also Available from Max Meyers . . .

RIDING THE HEAVENS
Stories and Adventures to Inspire Your Faith

Above the jungle slopes of Mount Bosavi, an airplane circles, its wings flashing in the equatorial sun. Descending to within feet of the treetops, it skims toward a clearing in the forest—then suddenly, from its cockpit, a small, bright object tumbles earthward . . . a can of paint. It is followed by another. And another. Call it the ultimate in special delivery. The Mission Aviation Fellowship (MAF) takes the gospel far beyond where the highway ends; the paint will help initiate contact with a newly discovered tribe in the hinterlands of Papua New Guinea. It's all in a day's work for Max Meyers—work he would trade for nothing else. What, after all, could ever equal the rewards of flying the good news of Christ's Kingdom to the world's rim?

In *Riding the Heavens,* Meyers shares with you unforgettable slices from his forty years as a missionary pilot: Moonrise at 35,000 feet in the cockpit of a jet fighter; medical help administered at arrow point; a night in a jungle lean-to with a cannibal-turned evangelist . . . this is no Hollywood script. It's the remarkable, true memoirs of a man who has known the drama, the humor, the tragedies, and the life-changing power of missions like few people ever know them. Sit in the pilot's seat and taste the panic of a mid-air "explosion"—and the comic relief that follows when you discover its source. Gaze across the expanse of mud that has buried a jungle village, including the missionary family who were your friends. Hold the hand of a dying boy and see him smile at you as he slips into the loving arms of Jesus.

And discover, above all, the faithfulness of the God of Jeshurun, "who rides on the heavens to help you, and on the clouds in his majesty." (Deut. 33:26) *Riding the Heavens* is a book of incredible adventures that will fuel your hunger to know God more deeply and experience his power and presence in your life.

Hardcover 0-310-23333-X

Pick up a copy at your favorite bookstore today!

ZONDERVAN